THE
WALL PILATES
— FOR —
SENIORS
BIBLE 7 IN 1

CLARA HANSON

Table of Contents

Dear Reader,

Welcome to the world of Wall Pilates for Seniors, a vibrant realm where the pages of this guide come alive with the promise of rejuvenation and strength. As the author of these words, I extend a heartfelt greeting to you, fellow traveler on this exhilarating journey.

Pilates, with its graceful movements and profound benefits, has the potential to transform not only your body but your entire outlook on life. In the following chapters, we'll delve into the realm of Wall Pilates, an approach specially crafted to cater to the unique needs and aspirations of seniors. Whether you're taking your initial steps into the world of Pilates or have been a longtime enthusiast, this guide offers a wealth of wisdom, exercises, and tailored routines to elevate your physical well-being and elevate your sense of self.

Yet, our voyage together is about much more than mere exercise. It's an exploration of the art of holistic well-being, a journey toward rediscovering your inner vitality and embracing the joys of an active life, no matter your age.

I'm here to be your guide, your motivator, and your companion on this path. Together, we'll unlock the potential of Wall Pilates to revitalize your body, rejuvenate your spirit, and celebrate the boundless vitality that accompanies your senior years.

With enthusiasm and warmth,

Clara

Book 1

Introduction to Wall Pilates for Seniors

Chapter 1

WHAT IS PILATES?

The Intriguing Journey of Pilates: From Recovery to Global Fame

In the early 1900s, Joseph Pilates, a German native born in 1883, crafted what we now recognize as the Pilates method. Growing up with ailments like asthma, rickets, and rheumatic fever, young Joseph was propelled by an unwavering determination to strengthen his fragile physique. His explorations led him to delve into yoga, martial arts, and gymnastics, weaving threads from each to craft his unique approach.

World War I found Joseph in the role of a nurse, where innovation met necessity. He designed bed-based exercises using springs and pulleys, confident that this system could help wounded soldiers rehabilitate more effectively than standard therapies of the time.

Post-war, the bustling streets of New York City beckoned, and Joseph set up his "Pilates Studio for Body Contrology." The city's elite, from dancers to athletes to Hollywood's shining stars, were soon devout followers. Joseph's teachings were clear: the journey to health necessitated proper alignment, controlled breathing, and a strong core.

Fast-forward to today, and Pilates enjoys a global fanbase. While the essence remains true to Joseph's original vision, it's a dynamic form of exercise, evolving yet rooted in its foundational principles. It's heralded for enhancing posture, boosting flexibility, and solidifying core strength.

Seniors, in particular, have embraced Pilates with open arms. Its gentle yet impactful nature allows for customization, offering an ideal fitness regimen for the golden years.

Yet, for all its widespread recognition, a veil of mystery cloaks Pilates. Myths and legends are intertwined with its history, leaving some puzzled about its essence.

Stay tuned as we next delve deeper into the myriad benefits of Pilates for seniors, differentiate it from other fitness forms, and guide you in embarking on your own Pilates journey with the right instructor.

Pilates for Seniors: Unlocking a World of Wellness

The golden years can shine even brighter when infused with the myriad benefits of Pilates. Tailored for every fitness level, Pilates promises physical rejuvenation and mental tranquility. Here's a snapshot of how seniors can thrive with Pilates:

Amplified Flexibility & Movement

Pilates gifts its practitioners with fluidity of movement. Its controlled, precise exercises stretch muscles, enhancing flexibility, and widening joint mobility. Everyday tasks, like reaching or bending, become more effortless, especially crucial for seniors facing age-related mobility challenges. And the best part? Pilates is adaptable, catering to everyone from beginners to flexibility mavens.

Bolstered Strength & Definition

Beyond just flexibility, Pilates is a powerhouse for holistic strength. It primarily targets the core – the abdominals, back, and pelvic muscles – but also sculpts arms, legs, and hips. The focus on alignment ensures optimal muscle engagement, all without the need for hefty weights, making it gentle on the joints.

Stand Tall: Improved Posture

Age might bring wisdom, but sometimes it also brings slouching. Pilates acts as a posture-corrector. By emphasizing a neutral spine and core engagement, it fortifies the muscles that keep you standing tall, countering age-related posture dips and associated pains.

Mental Oasis: Stress & Anxiety Relief

Pilates isn't just a body workout; it's a soul-soother. The exercises tether breath with movement, ushering in a meditative calm that banishes stress. Alongside the physical endorphin boost, the mindful nature of Pilates acts as a tranquil break from daily life's whirlwind.

Fortified Bones

Pilates' weight-bearing nature is a boon for bones, often vulnerable to density loss with age. Such exercises help counteract this natural decline, even potentially enhancing bone density. A study in the Journal of Women's Health Physical Therapy spotlighted postmenopausal women, revealing significant bone density upticks after Pilates sessions.

Heart's Delight: Cardiovascular Boost

Pilates might not be a heart-pounding cardio routine, but its benefits for the heart are undeniable. By aiding circulation and possibly lowering blood pressure, it's a silent hero for cardiovascular wellness.

Emotional Uplift

Beyond the tangible, Pilates cradles the spirit, boosting mood, self-worth, and a sense of tranquility.

The Unique Charm of Pilates for Seniors

Unleashing the Power of Mind–Body Connection

What sets Pilates apart from your typical workout? It's its uncanny ability to harmonize the mind and body. While most exercises zone in purely on muscle movement, Pilates introduces a dance between mental presence and physical motion. This practice encourages a deeper sense of self-awareness. By syncing breath with movement, you're not only toning your body but also cultivating inner peace, reducing anxiety, and elevating overall wellness.

The "Powerhouse" Core Focus

Ever heard of the "powerhouse"? In the world of Pilates, this refers to the core. The magic here is not just about sculpting abs but harnessing your body's central strength. For seniors, this is gold. As age might play tricks on our posture, targeting the core through Pilates can counterbalance these changes, reducing back pain, enhancing stability, and even upping your athletic game.

Mastering Movements: The Art of Control

Rush and hustle are not in Pilates' dictionary. Here, each motion is a deliberate act of art, emphasizing precision over pace. This not only builds strength and flexibility but also lessens injury risks. Think of it as moving with purpose and intention, benefiting especially seniors and those with balance concerns.

Friendly to All: Low-Impact Yet Impactful

Gone are the fears of jarring joints. Pilates' low-impact nature makes it a win for seniors and those in post-injury recovery. But don't be fooled – its gentleness packs a punch. Beyond being kind to joints, its alignment focus fortifies muscles around them, making it adaptable for any age or fitness level. Plus, there's a bonus: regular practice has been linked to boosted heart health and a serene state of mind.

Tailored to You: The Versatility of Pilates

One size doesn't fit all in Pilates. Its adaptable nature means it can serve a newbie, an athlete, or a senior alike. Whether you're at home, in a gym, or at a dedicated studio, Pilates molds to fit your pace and purpose, from rehab to athletic training or pure fitness.

Breathing Life into Exercise: The Power of Breath

If Pilates had a secret sauce, it would be the breath. This isn't your average inhale-exhale routine. Termed "lateral breathing", this technique saturates your body with oxygen, aiding movement and kindling a deeper mind-body bond. Benefits? Enhanced lung function, a calm mind, and for those with breathing conditions, a potential boost in respiratory health.

Pilates for Seniors: Mastering the Core Principles

The Essence of Pilates Pilates, at its heart, is a unique blend of proper alignment, breath synchronization, and mindful movement. These principles serve as the bedrock of the practice, culminating in a holistic fitness journey. Let's delve deeper into these guiding lights of Pilates.

1. Breath: More than Just Oxygen

Breathing in Pilates isn't only about oxygen intake; it's

a bridge between the mind and body. As practitioners harness their breath to guide their movements, they unlock a state of heightened awareness. This mindfulness not only clears mental fog but also curtails stress. Proper breathing activates core muscles, paving the way for stellar posture and minimizing injury risks. Beyond exercises, some even intertwine pranayama (yogic breath techniques) for enhanced lung function and meditative relaxation.

2. Concentration: The Mindful Link

The magic in Pilates often springs from focused attention. By grounding oneself in the present, one taps into enhanced movement control—ideal for injury recovery and chronic pain management. This deep focus ushers in tranquility, uplifting mood, and fostering body awareness, which in turn assists in pinpointing and rectifying imbalances.

3. Control: Precision in Motion

Pilates isn't about hasty repetitions. It champions slow, deliberate motions, ensuring utmost accuracy. This meticulousness bolsters balance and enhances stability. Beyond physical prowess, embracing control can be transformative, fostering discipline that transcends the mat and permeates daily life.

4. Centering: The Powerhouse Focus

Pilates zeroes in on our body's powerhouse—the core, encompassing the abdomen, lower back, and hips. By reinforcing these vital muscles, one achieves poised posture, minimizes back discomfort, and evens out body weight distribution. More than physical, centering fine-tunes mental focus, instilling a potent sense of self-confidence.

5. Precision: Detailing Every Move

Pilates is all about the details. Each motion is a testament to form and technique. Such rigorous precision not only maximizes physical rewards but enhances body cognizance and movement mastery. Moreover, it acts as an injury shield, preventing undue muscle or joint strain.

6. Flow: Dance of Movements

Pilates is akin to a dance, with seamless transitions and rhythmic movements, all in tune with one's breath. Such fluidity ensures optimal body functionality and wards off injuries. Beyond the physical, this graceful flow ushers in relaxation, melting away tension and potentially ushering practitioners into a serene meditative realm.

Wall's Guide to Pilates for the Golden Age

Your Body's Renewal Path through Pilates

Pilates isn't just an exercise; it's a journey—one that molds to your unique pace, strengths, and concerns. Let's dive into the diverse world of Pilates, tailoring each approach to the vibrant seniors who, like fine wine, only get better with time.

1. Mat Pilates: The Essentials

Picture this: you, a mat, and a realm of exercises waiting to be explored. Mat Pilates is your foundational playground, emphasizing core strength, flexibility, and balance. No fancy equipment here—just you leveraging your body's natural weight. Think of the 'Hundred'—a rhythmic arm pumping while your core engages—or the 'Roll Up', a graceful curl from lying down to sitting. These exercises cultivate deep connections with muscles you never knew you had, enhancing posture and breathing.

Golden Takeaway: Mat Pilates—uncomplicated, impactful, and crafted for everyone, especially seniors.

2. Reformer Pilates: Machine Magic

Welcome to the Reformer—a sleek apparatus that's more than meets the eye. This machine grants a blend of support and resistance, perfect for enhancing the familiar core-focused exercises of Pilates. Adjust the springs for tailored resistance, and embark on moves like the 'Footwork' or 'Rowing'. And for our golden-aged friends? The Reformer offers the stability needed to ensure confidence in every move.

Golden Takeaway: Reformer Pilates—the perfect balance of support and challenge, catering especially to those with balance concerns.

3. Tower Pilates: Rise High

The Tower, a magnificent vertical frame, brings a world of versatility. Attach springs or bars, and adapt each exercise to your level. Dive into the 'Leg Springs', or try 'Pull-Ups' for a core challenge. With the Tower's structure, seniors find an added layer of stability—making strength and bone density gains more accessible.

Golden Takeaway: Tower Pilates—versatility at its finest, supporting seniors in reaching their zenith.

4. Chair Pilates: Compact Powerhouse

A chair isn't just for sitting! Pilates introduces a specialized chair, turning balance and stability exercises into an art form. Engage in the 'Leg Press' or the rejuvenating 'Spine Stretch'. The chair's design supports those balance-challenged moments while introducing a fun balancing act of its own.

Golden Takeaway: Chair Pilates—compact, yet mighty, offering seniors the chance to master balance in new ways.

5. Cadillac Pilates: The Grand Stage

The Cadillac, or as some fondly call it, the trapeze table, is the grand stage of Pilates. With bars and springs galore, this equipment unlocks a spectrum of strength, flexibility, and coordination exercises. Seniors can safely engage in movements like the 'Leg Springs' and 'Roll-Downs', each catering to individual strengths and limitations.

Golden Takeaway: Cadillac Pilates—grandeur meets function, a sanctuary for seniors seeking comprehensive workouts.

Unlocking the Power of Pilates: Essential Gear Guide

Pilates, the exercise sensation that's captivated millions, thrives on its adaptability. Whether you're a minimalist, seeking strength with just a mat, or someone embracing the full studio experience, Pilates has equipment tailored to your journey. Let's dive into the essential gear that makes Pilates the transformative workout it is.

1. Pilates Mat: More than just a cushion, this foundational piece is your gateway into the world of Pilates. Crafted to support your body, its thickness and density are optimized for floor exercises, ensuring you're both comfortable and grounded.

2. Pilates Reformer: Imagine a sliding bed, but with springs, ropes, and a promise of a toned body. That's the reformer for you. Perfect for exercises ranging from beginner to pro, this dynamic machine offers resistance that amplifies every movement.

3. Pilates Cadillac: Dubbed the "Trapeze Table," this majestic equipment is more fun than it sounds. With an overhead frame decked out in ropes and pulleys, it's designed primarily for enhancing upper body strength and flexibility.

4. Pilates Chair: Compact but mighty, the Wunda Chair (its fancy name) features a seat with a spring-loaded pedal.

As you press and release, your legs, arms, and core are in for an effective workout.

5. Pilates Barrel: Resembling a curved wooden vault, this padded apparatus is ideal for stretches, backbends, and those coveted core routines.

6. Pilates Magic Circle: This isn't your ordinary ring. Often made from metal or rubber, it's designed to increase resistance in exercises. Whether you're squeezing it between your thighs or pressing with your hands, it's sure to add a little magic to your routine.

7. Pilates Ball: Bounce into balance with this inflatable sphere. Known for its core-enhancing capabilities, it also moonlights in stretching and balance drills, making it a versatile addition to any Pilates session.

In essence, Pilates is as simple or as intricate as you want it to be. Whether you're starting with just a mat or diving into the vast world of specialized gear, each piece of equipment is designed to sculpt, strengthen, and rejuvenate. So, roll out your mat or hop on that reformer - your Pilates transformation awaits.

Chapter 2

Introduction to Wall Pilates

Wall Pilates for Seniors: A Game-Changer in Healthy Aging

As a Wall Pilates trainer, I'm excited to introduce you to the wonders of Wall Pilates - a groundbreaking adaptation of the classic Pilates method, specifically designed for our golden years. This fitness regimen stands out, not just because of its unique use of the wall, but for the myriad of health benefits it offers.

Wall Pilates Demystified

At its core, Wall Pilates is all about leveraging a wall to make Pilates exercises accessible and effective for seniors. Traditional floor exercises might be daunting for some, especially those with balance or joint concerns. Enter Wall Pilates. The wall offers the support seniors need, letting them confidently engage in standing exercises, leg routines, and balance drills.

Why it works? The wall acts as a steadfast companion, offering both stability and security. Whether you're a newbie or an experienced fitness enthusiast, the wall ensures you get the most out of every movement.

Essentials to Kickstart Your Wall Pilates Journey:

- Comfortable Mat: A soft spot for some exercises and stretches.

- Yoga Block or Strap: To refine and enhance certain poses.

- Resistance Bands or Small Weights: Amp up the intensity as you progress.

Key Benefits Tailored for Seniors

Elevated Mobility: Aging can be tough on our joints. Wall Pilates targets those achy spots, particularly the spine, hips, and ankles. With improved flexibility, daily activities become a breeze, and risk of injury diminishes.

Boosted Strength: Did you know a study from the Journal of Aging and Physical Activity in 2014 spotlighted the strength-building capabilities of Pilates for older adults? Wall Pilates zeroes in on core, back, and legs, empowering seniors to conquer daily tasks effortlessly.

Posture Perfection: With age, we often slouch. Wall Pilates acts as the perfect antidote, enhancing spine-supporting muscles. Plus, a good posture uplifts mood, improves breathing, and even aids digestion.

Zen and the Art of Wall Pilates: Beyond physical perks, Wall Pilates doubles as a meditative practice. The concentration required nudges away daily stress, making way for tranquility.

Mastering Balance: Nothing is more critical than balance in our later years. Wall Pilates reinforces the muscles essential for stability, significantly reducing fall risks.

Heightened Body Awareness: Wall Pilates tunes you into your body's symphony. As you focus on alignment and engage even the tiniest muscles, you'll become more in sync with your body's needs and capabilities.

In conclusion, Wall Pilates is more than just an exercise— it's a lifestyle shift. It's about rejuvenating our golden years, making them truly glitter. So, seniors, grab that mat, find a wall, and let's get moving! Your body and mind will thank you.

Essential Gear for Elevating Your Wall Pilates Experience

Embarking on a Wall Pilates journey? Fantastic choice, especially for our golden agers seeking to rejuvenate their fitness. As an expert in Wall Pilates, I've got your back (literally and figuratively!). Here's a quick guide to the gear that can elevate your Wall Pilates experience:

- The Mighty Wall & Cozy Mat: At the heart of this practice is your trusted wall and a comfortable mat. These foundational elements provide the support and cushioning you'll need.

- Trusty Chair: Got balance concerns? A sturdy chair or

a stable surface within arm's reach is an ally for those seeking that extra layer of stability, especially when attempting new or challenging moves.

- Pilates Ball - Your Bouncy Buddy: Spice up your routines with a Pilates ball! Available in varied sizes, these balls not only inject fun into your workouts but also allow for targeted exercises for the core, legs, and arms.

- Resistance Bands - Flex Those Muscles: Wish to dial up the intensity? Resistance bands are your ticket. Available in varied resistance levels, they're perfect for customizing workouts. Whether you're a newbie or an advanced practitioner, there's a band out there with your name on it.

- Hand Weights for That Extra Oomph: For exercises that zoom in on the upper body, such as those tantalizing bicep curls or empowering shoulder presses, hand weights are magic. And guess what? They're available in diverse sizes, so you can pick what suits you best.

In a nutshell, Wall Pilates doesn't demand an arsenal of equipment. A few thoughtfully selected items are all you need. But remember, while the right tools can enhance your experience, the real magic lies in the moves and your commitment.

Chapter 3

Getting Started with Wall Pilates for Seniors

Safety First!

Venturing into any new exercise, especially as a senior, requires diligence. Always check with your healthcare professional to make sure Wall Pilates is suitable for your current health condition.

Finding Your Pace

When diving into Wall Pilates:

- Begin at Your Comfort Level: Start simple and ramp up intensity slowly. This gradual approach safeguards against injury and ensures consistent growth.

- Tune In: Your body knows best. If a movement feels off, adjust or take a momentary break. Pain is not a sign of progress; it's a cue to reassess.

Crafting Your Wall Pilates Sanctuary

- Location Matters: Opt for a quiet, well-lit area, free from distractions and potential tripping hazards.

- Stability is Key: A sturdy wall (or another steadfast surface) is essential. Ensure it's smooth and free of anything that might disturb your routine.

- Comfort Underfoot: A quality yoga or exercise mat cushions joints and ensures optimal form. Pick one that feels right—neither too thin nor too thick.

Essentials for Your Session:

- Dress for Success: Comfy and supportive attire enhances your workout experience.

- Stay Quenched: Hydration is vital. Have a water bottle at hand, and sip as needed. Remember, seniors may not always feel thirsty but still need to drink.

Stepping into the World of Wall Pilates

Choosing the right challenge level can feel daunting. If in doubt, a certified Pilates instructor or therapist can provide guidance. They'll consider your fitness journey, potential limitations, and end goals. As you grow stronger, don't be afraid to level up your exercises. But always circle back to listening to your body. It's a dance of challenge and respect.

In Conclusion

Embracing Wall Pilates is a journey. When approached with intention and safety in mind, it's a transformative tool for seniors—offering strength, balance, and mental clarity. Always pair your enthusiasm with a nod from your healthcare provider. With preparation and dedication, Wall Pilates can be a delightful addition to your wellness toolkit, regardless of age or fitness background.

Chapter 4

BASIC WALL PILATES EXERCISES

Begin with Brilliance: Wall Warm-Ups

Forget what you know about warm-ups. With Wall Pilates, it's not just a preamble but the golden key to making the most of your session. Crafted to be kind on those precious joints while setting the tempo, let's unveil the first act:

Wall Angels: Elevate Your Posture & Charge Your Upper Half

- Start Strong: Stand tall with your back against the wall, feet set hip-width apart. Extend your arms out at shoulder height, fingertips lightly brushing the wall.

- The Dance: Let your arms glide upwards, reaching for the sky, then gracefully lower them back to starting position. Remember, let the wall guide your movement; keep the connection.

- Golden Nugget: Resist any urge to arch your back. Power this movement with the might of your shoulders and upper back.

Wall Squats: Refine Those Legs & Stand Firm

- Start Strong: Stand with your back against the wall, feet set hip-width apart. Place your hands gently on your hips.

- The Dance: Slide down, imagining a hidden chair beneath you. Pause when your thighs level out, then rise, driven by the strength of your heels.

- Golden Nugget: Keep your back straight and steady. Watch those knees; ensure they don't jut beyond your toes.

Wall Push-ups: Craft a Robust Chest & Sculpted Arms

- Start Strong: Face the wall, hands pressed against it, just a bit wider than your sturdy shoulders. Step back a tad, imagine yourself on a slant.

- The Dance: Move towards the wall as if being pulled by a gentle wave, then drift back as the wave recedes.

- Golden Nugget: Maintain a straight line from the top of your head to your heels. Looking for a challenge? Adjust your hand spacing or change your angle to spice things up.

In the narrative of Wall Pilates, the wall isn't just a tool, but a collaborator. As chapters unfold, remember, it's a dance of discovery, personalization, and joy. So, embrace the journey, relish each step, and celebrate you!

Wall Pilates Exercises for Improving Core Strength and Stability

Core power isn't just about washboard abs—it's the unsung hero behind poised postures, graceful gaits, and the zestful vibrancy that defines our golden years. Through Wall Pilates, discover the secret alchemy to chisel this inner powerhouse, from the shield-like abdominals to the supporting chorus of back and pelvic players.

Wall Planks: The Architect of Core Mastery

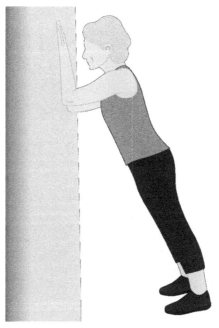

- Initiate: Stand proudly facing the wall. Place your hands on it, aligned with your shoulders.

- Engage: Step your feet back, forming a strong, straight line from your head to your heels, your arms leading the way forward.

- Hold & Conquer: Engage your core deeply, breathing steadily, and bask in the strength emanating from your center.

- Graceful Exit: Step your feet back towards the wall, standing upright and celebrating your accomplishment.

Golden Guidance: Ensure a consistent line of energy, evading any dips or peaks in your form. Feel a tad more daring? Shift hand placement or opt for formidable forearms on the wall.

Wall Sit-Ups: The Abdominal Artisan

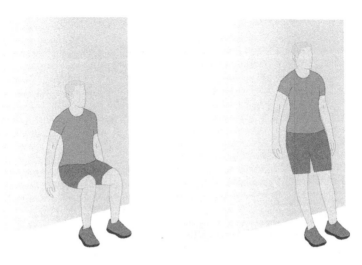

- Initiate: Sit with your back against the wall, knees bent at a 90-degree angle, and those feet grounded on the floor. Place your hands either crossed on your chest or supporting your head.

- Engage: Activate your core muscles and slowly curl forward, lifting your upper body. As you rise, ensure there's space between your chin and chest.

- Descend with Decorum: Gracefully return to your starting position, preparing for the next upward movement.

Golden Guidance: Neck's grace is paramount. Abandon any neck tugs, seeking power from the belly's depths and moving with purpose.

Wall Twists: The Torsional Tailor of Abdominals & Obliques

- Initiate: Stand facing the wall, feet hip-width apart. Extend arms straight ahead at shoulder height, with palms gently touching the wall.

- Engage: Pivot on your right foot, and move your left arm in a wide arc towards the right, as if drawing on the wall.

- Recalibrate: Come back to the starting position with both arms extended forward.

- Alternate's Art: Now, pivot on your left foot and let your right arm swing in a wide arc towards the left wall.

Golden Guidance: The twist's essence is in the torso's

rotation, not just arm theatrics. Like a well-oiled door hinge, the movement is smooth, back remains dignified, and the core conducts the symphony.

Embrace these exercises as the choreography of your core's renaissance. With each repetition, remember: Wall Pilates isn't just movement; it's a poetic dialogue between you and the wall. Enjoy the dance!

Wall Pilates Exercises for Improving Flexibility and Range of Motion

Embrace the wall as your stretching buddy. These exercises dance between the upper and lower realms of your body, creating a harmonious blend of flexibility and freedom.

Heart-to-Wall Embrace (Chest Stretch)

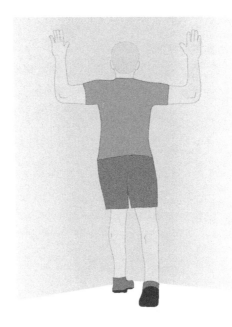

- Position: Stand with arms spread out, palms touching the wall at shoulder height.

- Action: Slowly lean forward, letting your chest stretch.

- Duration: Hold this stretch for 10-15 seconds.

Calf Crescent (Calf Stretch)

- Position: Stand slightly leaning forward, hands straight out at shoulder level.

- Action: Step forward into a soft lunge, ensuring the back leg remains straight and grounded.

- Duration: Hold the stretch for 10-15 seconds, then switch to the other leg.

Ballet Quad Poise (Quad Stretch)

- Position: Stand facing the wall, left hand lightly touching it for balance.

- Action: Gently bend your right leg, bringing your heel close to your butt.

- Duration: Hold this balanced position for 10-15 seconds before switching to the other side.

Golden Mantra: Embrace the stretch, feel the rhythm, but never push to the point of pain. Think of it as a dance; it should flow, not jolt.

Wall Lunges

Dream of toned legs and strong posture even as the years advance? Dive into Wall Lunges! This sassy Pilates exercise zones in on your quads, hamstrings, and glutes, giving them the love they need.

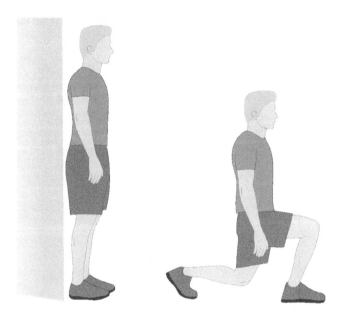

How to Get It Right:

- Strike your stance with the wall as your backdrop, feet relaxed and hip-width apart, hands poised on your hips.

- Unleash the diva within: confidently step one foot out, and as if you're hitting a dance move, bend both knees gracefully. The back knee nearly kisses the floor, and the front knee stays shy, stacked right over your ankle.

- Hold that fierce lunge when your front thigh aligns with

the floor, then spring back to your opening position.

- Ride that rhythm a couple more beats, then switch it up, letting the other leg steal the show.

Pro Tip: Own your posture! Keep it sleek and straight, letting those leg muscles do their thing. Ensure your weight plays fair, balancing between your front and back foot.

Heavenly Heels (Hamstring Stretch)

Looking to flex some flexibility? Your hamstrings, the elegant muscles painting the back of your thighs, crave this Wall Pilates classic.

Steps to Hamstring Bliss:

- Settle in: Lie back and wiggle those hips close to the wall, letting your legs reach skyward.

- Embrace the sensation as you smoothly slide your heels down, keeping your legs as straight as the horizon. When the back of your thighs sing with a stretch, you've struck gold.

- Relish that rich feeling for 20-30 seconds.

- Want to up the ante? Nudge your buttocks just a smidge closer to the wall.

- Elegantly rise, guiding your heels back up, resetting to your starting position.

- Give it another whirl, or maybe even two, following your own rhythm.

Remember: Deep, harmonious breaths are your best friend. Keep your back's integrity, ensuring it doesn't curve or arch. The aim? A glorious hamstring stretch sans pain. If any discomfort crashes the party, bow out gracefully. Safety first!

Cool-down Wall Exercises

Just knocked out that Wall Pilates routine? Fabulous! Now, let's coast into the soothing world of post-Pilates cooldown. Easing your muscles back to their relaxed state is essential. Not only does it help fend off the dreaded post-workout soreness, but it also keeps injuries at bay.

Here's your ticket to the ultimate relaxation:

Wall stetches

Ever dreamt of legs that just go on forever? Here's a sweet taste of that.

Strut Your Stuff:

- Plant yourself in front of the wall, feet casually spaced hip-width apart.

- Stretch it out, with hands connecting to the wall roughly at shoulder height.

- Now, add a little flair: gracefully step one foot back – about the length of a dance step (two feet) away from the wall. Let the heel find the floor, while the toes point up towards the heavens.

- As the front knee dips, lean in and enjoy the beautiful stretch unfolding in your hamstring and calf.

- Relish in that peaceful stretch for 30 seconds, then switch to let the other side shine.

Golden Rule: Own that posture! Your back should rival a ruler in its straightness. As your muscles whisper their tales of stretch, remember – pain's not part of this narrative.

Wall calf stretch

This Pilates gem is all about giving some TLC to those calf muscles that support you, day in and day out.

Here's the Groove:

- Face the wall, hands comfortably resting at shoulder height.

- Take a step back with one foot, heel anchored, toes pointing ahead.

- Bend the front knee, leaning towards the wall, ensuring the tale of the back leg remains straight.

- Hold this calf-caressing position for 30 seconds, then switch sides for an encore with the other leg.

Pro-tip: Keep your spine sleek, heels rooted, and shoulders melt away from your ears. Any discomfort? Put a pin in that move and check in with a health guru.

Wall tricep stretch

Give a nod to the unsung hero of your arms: the triceps. Let's get them feeling all kinds of limber.

Move to the Beat:

- Kick off facing the wall, feet nonchalantly spaced hip-width apart. Hands? They're up, high-fiving the wall at shoulder level.

- Take a step back, cinema-style, arms extending until your body slants gracefully.

- Lower yourself, elbows bending, until you're almost cheek-to-cheek with the wall.

- Relish in that stretch for a good 15-30 seconds, then

strut back up to your starting stance.

Star Tip: Picture yourself sandwiched between two panes of glass – staying straight is the game. That stretch should be a lullaby, not a scream. Discomfort? Tap out and seek pro advice.

Chapter 5

ELEVATE YOUR WALL PILATES GAME

Congratulations! Having mastered the Wall Pilates fundamentals, you're primed to step into the elite arena. This chapter unveils a series of more ambitious moves tailor-made for seasoned seniors hungry for a touch more zest in their routine.

Advanced Engagements for the Experienced

Each of these dynamic workouts is a sophisticated spin on the foundational exercises, beckoning greater muscular prowess and poise. Let's dive in!

Wall Plank with Leg Lift:

Rev up your core strength, balance, and stability with this chic variation.

- Square up with the wall, body in a plank stance—hands casually positioned at shoulder height, feet set hip-width apart.

- Fire up your core and smoothly lift one leg, keeping it straight as an arrow, parallel to the ground.

- Give it a moment to hover, then gracefully lower it.

- Switch gears and give the other leg its time to shine.

- Flow through, switching legs, and always bear in mind: maintain a sleek, unbroken line with your body, free of any sagging or arching.

Wall Push-up with Knee Tuck

Here's a ritzy workout mingling the elegance of a push-up with the flair of a knee tuck.

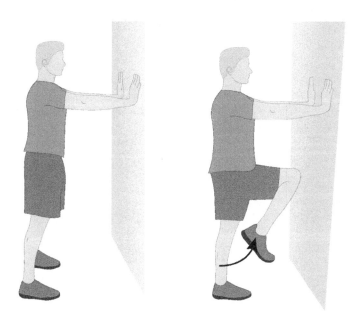

The Performance:

- Stand confidently facing the wall, hands casually set shoulder width apart and at shoulder height. Your body—striking a straight line from head to heels.

- Gracefully step back a few paces, transitioning into a plank.

- Engage your core and lean into the wall, bringing your chest closer.

- As you gracefully return to your starting position, draw

your right knee up, letting it tease your chest.

- For your next move, let the left leg take center stage.

And hey, if today's not your day for the full routine, go halfsies with the knee-grounded push-up. It's all about the journey.

Wall Sit-up with Twist

Combine the classical sit-up's charm with a twist's panache.

The Steps:

- Lean against the wall, feet planted and hip-width apart, looking as if you're waiting for a grand announcement.

- With arms folded as if holding a royal secret, use your core strength to rise majestically.

- At the peak of your lift, add a noble twist, making sure your lower realm stays steady.

- Gracefully settle back down, prepared to showcase the same elegance to the other side.

Remember, throughout this choreography, wear your posture like a crown, safeguarding your regality, and never rushing through the moves. After all, in Wall Pilates, every move is a masterpiece in its own right.

Balance & Coordination with Wall Pilates

In the dance of life, balance and coordination play starring roles. Wall Pilates offers seniors the golden ticket to hone these vital attributes while also gifting muscles with newfound strength. Here's a peek into some star moves:

Wall Single Leg Balance

This move isn't just about balance; it's about finesse.

How it's done:

- Stand facing the wall, feet together and hands confidently at shoulder level on the wall.

- Strike your best flamingo pose: lift one foot, letting the other take center stage. A tiny bend in the standing knee and an engaged core are your sidekicks.

- Maintain this for 30 seconds, then switch feet for an encore.

- Want to spice things up? Close your eyes or lessen your

hand's touch on the wall for an extra challenge.

- Always flaunt impeccable posture, and lean into the wall just enough to feel supported, not reliant.

Wall Lunge with Knee Lift

Marrying balance, power, and grace, this exercise also gifts your legs with a sweet burn.

The Choreography:

- Begin by standing tall facing the wall, hands elegantly placed at shoulder height.

- With finesse, step one foot back, making sure your front knee dreams of aligning directly above the ankle.

- Sink into a lunge, led by the front knee, while maintaining your back leg straight and noble.

- Rise triumphantly, pulling your back knee forward in a majestic arc, your core acting as the anchor.

- Hold that stately position for a moment, then ease back to your starting stance.

- Repeat this graceful sequence a few times, then switch to let the other leg take the lead.

Wall Squat with Calf Raise

A hearty nod to the powerhouses of the lower body, this move is where quads, glutes, and calves shine.

Steps to Stardom:

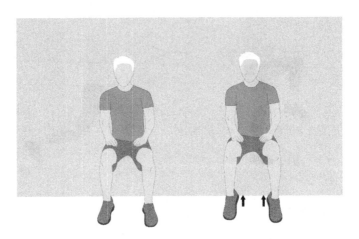

1. Position yourself against the wall, with feet spread as wide as your shoulders. Take a small step forward, ensuring you're not pressed too closely to the wall.

2. Lower yourself into a squat position as if you're about to sit on an invisible chair, stopping when your thighs are level with the ground.

3. While in this squat, lift your heels off the ground, standing on your tiptoes.

4. Hold for a moment, then place your heels back down and stand up.

5. For added support, place a cushion or ball between your lower back and the wall.

Elevate Your Strength with Wall Pilates

Our walls, often overlooked, are actually the secret to unlocking a stronger, fitter you. Wall Pilates has brilliantly choreographed moves that not only amplify your strength and fitness but also become a playground for your core. Let's unveil these power-packed routines:

Wall Pike

Designed for the ambitious, the Wall Pike is your ticket to sculpting the core, shoulders, and hamstrings.

The Moves:

1. Start in a plank position with hands on the ground and feet against the wall.
2. Slide your feet up the wall while lifting your hips, forming an upside-down V shape.
3. Hold at the top for a moment, pressing your heels down and engaging your core.
4. Return to the plank position. Repeat as desired.
5. Keep your core tight and shoulders relaxed. Be mindful

of your neck and back, and don't push too hard.

Wall Mountain Climbers

Imagine you're on the Rockies, with each rep. This routine invites the core, upper, and lower body to the party.

Scaling the Heights:

1. Start in a plank position with your feet on the ground and hands against the wall.
2. Activate your core and lift one knee up toward your chest, keeping the other foot firmly planted.
3. Switch legs, moving back and forth like you're climbing.
4. Maintain a consistent speed and keep your body straight like a board.
5. Do as many repetitions as you'd like.
6. Keep your hips level and back straight. Ensure your shoulders are above your hands. For an extra challenge, move faster or bring your knee closer to your chest.

Wall Single Leg Deadlift

A balletic motion that's less dance, more power; it's a toast to the glutes, hamstrings, and the muscles of the lower back.

Steps to Grace:

1. Position yourself facing the wall, feet set hip-width apart, and place your hands on the wall aligned with your shoulders.

2. Lift one foot straight back, keeping it level with the ground. Lean forward with your upper body until it's parallel to the floor.

3. Pause when your body is flat, then return to the starting position and place the lifted foot down.

4. Repeat the movement, then switch to the other foot.

5. Keep a soft bend in the leg you're standing on. Engage your core and keep your back straight. For added comfort, use a cushion or yoga block under the

standing foot.

The Wall's Embrace – Cool Down and Stretch

The grand finale of every workout deserves a calm yet impactful curtain call. In the world of Wall Pilates, our trusted wall once again proves its prowess, guiding us through serene stretches that rejuvenate and revitalize post-workout. Let's delve into some wall-assisted cool-down classics!

Wall Chest Stretch:

A trifecta targeting the chest, shoulders, and arms.

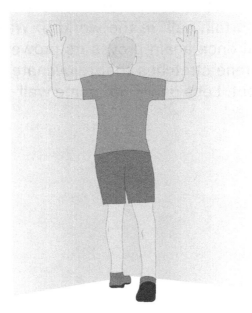

Guided Steps:

1. Stand in front of the wall with your feet spaced hip-width apart. Extend your arms and place your hands on the wall.

2. Step forward with one foot, bending your elbows and leaning towards the wall while keeping your back straight.

3. Hold this stretch for 20-30 seconds.

4. Step back and repeat with the other foot.

Pro-tip: If your 9-to-5 has you desk-bound, this can be your mini-refresh throughout the day. Always honor your body's cues; if something feels off, adjust.

Wall Shoulder Stretch:

Elevate shoulder flexibility with this gentle yet potent stretch.

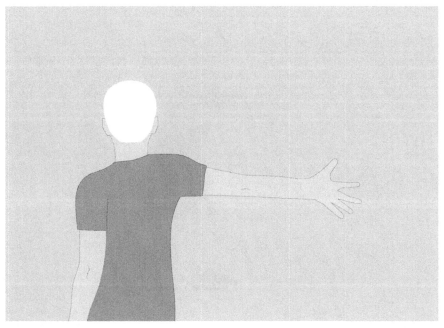

Guided Steps:

1. Stand sideways to the wall, an arm's length away.

2. Place the closest hand on the wall, fingers pointing up.

3. Turn your body away from the wall, stretching your shoulder.

4. Hold for 15-30 seconds, then switch sides.

Advanced Nuance: Edge your arm slightly higher on the wall, deepening the stretch. Regular rendezvous with this stretch can usher in fluid shoulder movements and ward off stiffness.

Wall Calf Stretch:

A salve for those ever-working calf muscles.

Guided Steps:

Place your hands on the wall at shoulder height.

Step one foot back, pressing the heel down firmly.

Lean slightly forward, bending the front knee, while feeling the stretch in the calf of the back leg.

Hold for 15-30 seconds, then switch legs.

Golden Rule: Maintain alignment - straight back, squared

hips, and forward-facing feet. If your calf craves a deeper stretch, step back a tad more. However, pain is never the goal.

Wrap Up Thoughts

Your body is a finely-tuned instrument, deserving of attention and care. These stretches are its loving encore. Embrace them with form over volume. And remember, as with any beautiful journey, Wall Pilates progression is laced with consistent practice and heartfelt patience. Cheers to your ever-evolving fitness narrative!

Chapter 6

The Power of Persistence

Mastering Wall Pilates

Unlocking the treasure trove of Wall Pilates is akin to embarking on an invigorating journey. Rich in rewards, it promises enhanced strength, nimbleness, and equilibrium. Yet, like any voyage, maintaining zest and advancing can sometimes feel like an uphill battle. Here's the compass to navigate with purpose and zest:

Crafting Intent

- Dream, But Dream Smart: Begin with visions, but mold them into realistic milestones. Revel in the triumphs, no matter how minute, and see any hiccup not as a setback but a setup for a comeback.

- Commit to Consistency: Carve out your Wall Pilates moments daily. A slice of dedicated time, even if it's just a few heartbeats, beats a sporadic approach.

- Pilates Partnerships: Teaming up with a pal or kin amplifies the fun and fuels commitment. It's mutual motivation with a dash of friendly accountability.

- Refresh and Revive: Routine is comforting, but

occasionally shaking up your Wall Pilates repertoire can keep things lively and intriguing.

- Hear Your Body's Whispers: Pace yourself. If your body murmurs for a pause, heed its wisdom. Resilience is about harmony, not strain.

Pilates Pitfalls – Dodge 'Em

- The Allure of Perfect Form: A masterpiece is crafted with precision. Engage muscles mindfully and steer clear of shortcuts or misalignments.

- Eagerness vs. Overzealousness: In your enthusiasm, don't overshadow the core principle: gradual progression. Rushing is the foe of mastery.

- Diverse is Dynamic: Wall Pilates is stellar, but dance with other fitness modalities too. Blend in cardio, muscle toning, and limbering stretches.

Daily Wall Pilates Integration

- Warm-Up Wonders: Prior to diving into Wall Pilates, invigorate your muscles with supple stretches and a touch of cardio.

- Sacred Spaces: Designate a serene corner for your practice, an oasis where focus flourishes and motivation blooms.

- Prop Power: Using props like yoga blocks or straps isn't just about modification. They're tools to tailor exercises to your unique rhythm.

- Journal Your Journey: Chronicle your Wall Pilates adventures. Not just as a measure of progress, but as a testament to your dedication.

Marching forth with these insights, your Wall Pilates expedition can only amplify in joy and benefits. Honor yourself, cherish the strides, and above all, revel in the holistic wellness that unfolds. Here's to your Pilates-powered voyage!

Chapter 7

Your Top Queries Answered

Embarking on the Wall Pilates journey, especially as a senior, can be brimming with curiosity and a pinch of trepidation. It's only natural to have a few queries before diving in. Let's navigate these waters together, dispelling doubts and bolstering confidence!

Q: Can seniors safely embrace Wall Pilates?

A: Absolutely! Wall Pilates is crafted to be senior-friendly. However, as with any new venture, take it one step at a time and stay in tune with your body's signals. If you've got specific health histories or conditions, a quick chat with your healthcare provider before beginning is a good rule of thumb.

Q: What if walls are scarce in my space? Any alternatives?

A: Certainly! While walls amplify the experience, they aren't exclusive. Modified versions exist for many exercises. Think squats or lunges sans wall, or even utilizing a sturdy chair for some extra support.

Q: What's the optimal frequency for Wall Pilates sessions?

A: Aim to get moving for about 30 minutes daily, spanning at least 5 days a week. If a full session feels overwhelming, sprinkle shorter ones throughout your day. As your Wall Pilates prowess grows, you can play around with increasing either your session lengths or frequency.

Q: Fashion or function – what's the dress code for Wall Pilates?

A: Go for function! Don outfits that are comfy and airy, ensuring freedom in every twist and turn. Steer clear of too-loose attire that might play spoilsport during your sessions.

Q: Motivation dips are real! How can I keep the Wall Pilates flame alive?

A: Set your sights on achievable milestones and revel in every achievement. A workout buddy or group class can sprinkle some fun and camaraderie. Infuse variety in your sessions, experimenting with fresh routines to keep your engagement levels peaked.

Q: Ouch, that hurts! What if I face discomfort during my exercises?

A: Halt right there! If an exercise sparks pain or unease, pause and gauge the situation. Your body's cues are invaluable. If discomfort lingers or escalates, it's best to consult a healthcare professional.

Wall Pilates, with its myriad benefits, awaits your exploration. By addressing these questions head-on, you're setting the stage for a safe, enjoyable, and transformative experience. Dive in with awareness, savor the process, and watch as Wall Pilates rejuvenates and strengthens you, one session at a time!

Chapter 8

A New Chapter of Wellness

Kudos to you for diving into the transformative world of Wall Pilates for seniors! Each stretch, each motion, and every breath you've embraced on this journey has advanced you towards a fitter, more radiant version of yourself. Now, let the magic of maintaining a stellar form amplify those benefits.

Your Next Steps: Exploring Beyond the Wall

The world of fitness is expansive, offering a plethora of avenues to explore:

- Community Connections: Consider dipping your toes into a local fitness circle or enrolling in a specialized class nearby. The camaraderie might just spice up your routine!

- Digital Dive: From enlightening YouTube tutorials to intuitive fitness apps, there's a digital guru for everyone. Dive deep, explore, and tailor your regimen.

Spotlight: 'Chair Yoga for Seniors' by Helen Stone

For those looking to blend serenity with strength, Helen Stone's 'Chair Yoga for Seniors' is a gem. Embracing a tranquil, low-impact yoga style, it's all about achieving mindfulness and flexibility right from your chair. Its step-by-step guide, laced with adaptive modifications, pairs seamlessly with your Wall Pilates repertoire, ensuring an all-rounded fitness approach.

You can get it by scanning the following QR Code:

In conclusion, fitness isn't a chapter, it's an unfolding story. Your dedication, coupled with consistent efforts, is the secret sauce to a life brimming with strength, agility, and boundless energy. Onward and upward!

Book 2

Standing
Wall Pilates
for Seniors

Chapter 1

DISCOVERING STANDING WALL PILATES FOR SENIORS

Enter the transformative world of Standing Wall Pilates: a gentle exercise tailored for seniors, serving as a beacon for enhancing balance, flexibility, and strength. With the dependable support of a wall, this practice empowers seniors to traverse from delicate stretches to dynamic movements. The brilliance? Achieving all this in the embrace of correct form, minimizing injury odds. Beyond the physical, Standing Wall Pilates is a posture-perfector, an essential ingredient for robust mobility and sidestepping falls. Bonus? It's a joint's best friend, providing relief by distributing pressure, ensuring every senior basks in amplified health and vibrancy.

Why Standing Wall Pilates is a Senior's Best Friend

- Balancer & Guardian: Age can be mischievous, often trying to tip our balance. But with Wall Pilates, combat this mischief by fortifying muscles, significantly reducing fall probabilities.

- Posture & Powerhouse Booster: With the wall's unwavering support, your core gets a workout of its own, ensuring an erect posture while nurturing your spine's health.

- Flexibility's Friend: Time can sometimes stiffen our joints, but Standing Wall Pilates acts as the perfect counter, preserving joint flexibility and keeping rigidity at bay.

- Strength Sans Strain: Bid goodbye to heavy weights. This Pilates variant leverages one's body weight, sculpting strength without overtaxing joints.

- Mind & Mood Lifter: More than muscle-deep, Standing Wall Pilates can be a balm for the soul, diminishing stress, and honing mental agility. Dive in, and witness a surge in mood, cognitive prowess, and memory.

In essence, no matter your fitness panorama, Standing Wall Pilates is a stellar pick for holistic wellness.

Your Standing Wall Pilates Toolkit

Kickstarting your Standing Wall Pilates journey demands minimal gear:

- The Basics: A cushioning yoga mat, attire that celebrates movement, and, of course, a steadfast wall.

- Level Up: As you delve deeper, consider resistance bands or petite weights to spice things up.

Elevate Your Experience:

- Roll with it: A foam roller isn't just a tension-easer; it's versatile, aiding certain exercises.

- Blocks & Cushions: For those exercises demanding a touch more comfort, a yoga block or cushion can be your best ally.

As you evolve in your practice, toys like balls and bands can amplify your sessions, targeting distinct muscles. Remember, the mantra is form over force, always!

Up next? A spectrum of Standing Wall Pilates exercises, crafted with seniors in mind. Whether you're a newbie or a Pilates aficionado, our curated guide promises enhanced strength, impeccable balance, and a sprightly you.

Chapter 2

The Perfect Prelude: Warm-Up Drills

The Vitality of a Proper Warm-Up

Like an overture to an opera, a warm-up sets the tone for what's to come. Especially for our seasoned generation, ensuring the body is gracefully prepped safeguards against strains, guaranteeing a seamless segue into the Standing Wall Pilates sequence. Ready to dive in? Here are some senior-friendly warm-ups tailored for Wall Pilates.

Shoulder Rolls: Mobilizing the Upper Back

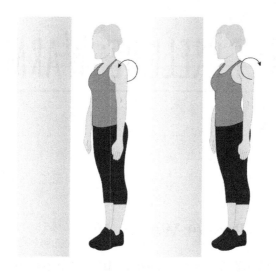

- Position: Stand parallel to the wall, feet planted hip-width. Hands? Gracefully place them on the wall, aligning with your shoulders.

- Action: Envision drawing circles with your shoulders - roll them forward, lift a tad, take them back, then gently lower. Ten times, then swap directions.

- Golden Nuggets: It's all in the shoulder blades; let them dance. But a gentle reminder — no shrugging. Keep those ears and shoulders distant!

- Customize It: If shoulder mobility isn't your forte, embrace smaller arcs, or nix the backward arc.

Leg Swings: Energizing the Lower Limbs

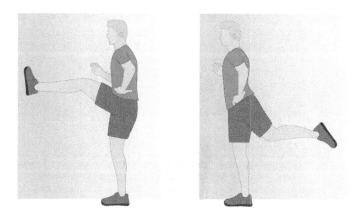

- Position: Face the wall, hands serenely on it, aligned with your hips.

- Action: Let one leg sweep forth and back, like a pendulum, ensuring it remains poised. Ten sweeps and it's the other leg's turn!

- Golden Nuggets: Picture a tree – solid trunk, swaying branches. Be that tree. Your torso remains rooted while your leg oscillates.

- Customize It: Balance feeling shaky? Grab a chair or clutch a countertop.

Arm Circles: Giving Wings to Your Shoulders

- Position: Stand akin to a starfish – feet hip-width apart and arms extending sideways at shoulder elevation.

- Action: Let your arms waltz – circle them forward, elevate slightly, reverse, then dip. Ten graceful twirls, then let's reverse the route.

- Golden Nuggets: Think elegance, not effort. Relax those shoulders and let the upper back muscles lead this dance.

- Customize It: If your shoulders are a tad rusty, embrace cozier circles or skip the skyward move.

Squat with Overhead Reach: Total Body Tune-Up

- Position: Feet stationed a smidge more than hip-width. As for the arms? Reach for the skies!

- Action: Imagine sitting in an invisible chair. As you descend, keep those knees neighborly with toes. Rise and repeat, for ten.

- Golden Nuggets: Visualize a puppet string pulling you from your crown. Stay lofty. And those knees? No inward parties!

- Customize It: If squats aren't your jam, try a demi-squat or just keep those arms by your side.

Remember, this warm-up isn't just a precursor – it's the bedrock of your Standing Wall Pilates expedition. Prioritize alignment, cherish technique, and never shy away from tailoring moves. Every journey is unique; make this one distinctly yours!

Chapter 3

POSTURE PERFECTION

The Power of Posture

Posture is the unsung hero of our well-being. Especially in our golden years, letting it slip can unlock a Pandora's box of discomfort. Enter Standing Wall Pilates, your savior for stellar alignment. Let's dive into some wall-infused exercises that champion great posture.

The Wall Angel – Your Upper Body's Guardian

The Wall Angel isn't just another exercise – it's your ticket to sculpted posture and renewed mobility.

- Set-Up: Align yourself with the wall – heels, hips, shoulders, and noggin should all share a moment with it. Raise those arms to shoulder level, bending the elbows at 90 degrees, palms greeting the world.

- Flow: Elevate your arms, making the wall their dance partner. Reach as high as possible without your back trying to escape. A moment at the zenith, then let them glide down.

- Key Takeaways: Shoulders down! Let your upper back muscles do the heavy lifting. Experiencing a pinch? Adjust as needed. Want some spice? A resistance band or a wee weight can up the ante.

Wall Press - Boosting Your Brawn

The Wall Press isn't just about strength; it's a recipe for a chiseled chest and toned arms.

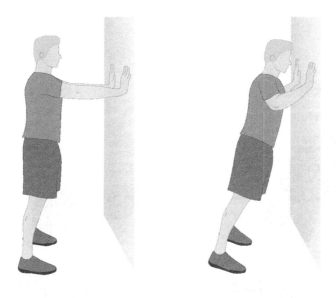

- Set-Up: Facing the wall, stretch those arms out, hands planted firmly at shoulder height.

- Flow: Engage your core, then lean into the wall till your nose teases a touch. A momentary pause, then reclaim your start.

- Key Takeaways: Core is king – keep it tight. Shoulders? Relaxed. Breathing? Essential. Starting? Take it slow and work your way up.

Wall Squat – The Lower Body Love Affair

The Wall Squat is more than a workout – it's a love letter to your legs.

- Set-Up: Stand with your back to the wall, ready for action.

- Flow: Descend into a squat, envisioning an invisible chair. Seek thighs parallel to the ground, then return to the throne.

- Key Takeaways: Your back? A pillar of straightness. Weight? Balanced. Starting depth? Shallow, progressing deeper over time. Got knee twinges? Scale back or consult a health expert.

Nifty Tweaks

- Wall Angel: Opt for smaller arm movements or add light resistance for more zest.

- Wall Press: Modify the distance from the wall or use an incline surface. Craving more? More reps or light weights can do the trick.

- Wall Squat: Adjust squat depth for discomfort, or employ a cushion for added support. Resistance bands around thighs can amp up alignment or add challenge.

Final Wisdom: Technique and alignment are your best buddies. Embrace them. Befriend modifications and tailor exercises to your groove. As you dance with these routines, you'll not only enhance posture but also craft a holistic well-being narrative. Your Standing Wall Pilates journey is not just about the destination; relish every step.

Chapter 4

MASTERING BALANCE AND STABILITY

The Essence of Balance

For our seasoned champions out there, balance is more than just standing tall; it's a key to safety and grace. With our trusty wall, let's embark on a transformative journey to be rock-steady, one exercise at a time.

Single Leg Stand – The Art of Poise

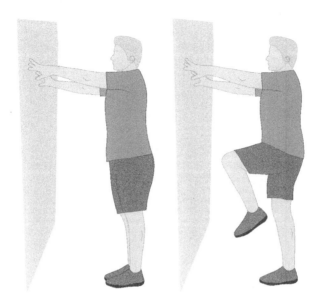

- Set-Up: Square up to the wall, hands at shoulder height for assurance.

- Flow: Shift and elevate! Let the right foot rise while the left foot grounds you. Own this posture for 10-20 seconds, then swing it the other way.

- Spice It Up: Feeling brave? Close those peepers and test your equilibrium.

Golden Nuggets:

- Square hips, locked gaze, and an active core are your trio to triumph.

- Soft surfaces like yoga mats add a touch of safety.

- Adjust your challenge – it's okay to keep both feet on

terra firma initially.

Lateral Leg Lift – Sideways Elevation

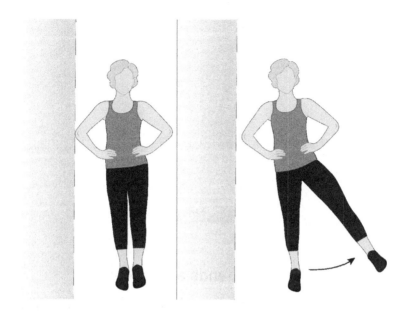

- Set-Up: Sidle up to the wall. Hands ready, stance set.
- Flow: Defying gravity, let the left leg rise, keeping it arrow-straight. A brief hold, then reunion with the floor. Flip sides after a set.

Golden Nuggets:

- Steady trunk, no leaning allowed!
- A slight bend or reduced lift is A-okay. Remember, it's your journey.
- Chair or table by your side? Perfect for that added confidence boost.

Heel-to-Toe Walk – The Balance Ballet

- Set-Up: Greet the wall, hands at the ready.

- Flow: Dance forward! Right heel kisses the toes of the left foot, then swap as you keep the flow.

Golden Nuggets:

- Eyes forward, captain! It anchors your balance.

- In moments of wobble, short steps or a mini-pause can bring you back.

- If standing tall tires you out, enlist the aid of a trusty chair.

In A Nutshell: Wall Pilates is not just a set of exercises; it's a dialogue with your body. By tuning in and adjusting as needed, you elevate your sense of balance and stability. Whether you're acing it or taking baby steps, remember – every movement is a celebration of progress. Rock on, balance maestro!

Golden Rules for Balance and Stability Mastery

Embarking on the dance of balance? Remember, we're all on unique journeys. Here's your roadmap to stability success:

- Start Smart: Embrace exercises that gel with your current groove. As your confidence swells, up the ante.

- Wall Wisdom: While our trusty wall stands ready to support, challenge yourself to occasionally let go. It's like teaching a kid to ride a bike - at first, they need training wheels, and over time, they'll ride freely.

- Breathe Easy: Let your breath be your rhythm. As you exhale, imagine releasing tension and inhale the strength to stand tall.

- Core Central: Think of your core as your internal anchor. Engage it, and let it guide your posture to perfection.

- Listen to Your Dance Partner (Your Body!): Feeling off-beat? Pause. There's no shame in resting and retrying. After all, the best dancers know when to take a breather.

Tailoring Your Balance Journey

Our bodies are like snowflakes - unique and wondrous. So, here are some tweaks to ensure your balance exercises resonate with you:

- Balance Buddies: For those wanting a bit more support, sturdy chairs or countertops can be your dance partners.

- Eyes Wide Shut: Ready for an advanced move? Test your balance prowess with closed eyes. But remember, safety first!

- Surfing on Land: Craving a challenge? Simulate ocean waves beneath your feet with an unstable surface like a foam pad. It's a beach day, minus the sunburn!

- Safety Serenade: Pilates is like music – soothing and rejuvenating. But, always jam with a healthcare pro's advice, especially if past hiccups, like falls or injuries, have played their tune. Let's ensure our balance journey is both fun and safe!

Chapter 5

COOL-DOWN EXERCISES

As the final act of your Standing Wall Pilates session, easing into cool-down exercises helps return your body to its peaceful haven. It's the curtain call your body cherishes after a fabulous performance. Let's dive into a trio of soul-soothing stretches.

The Graceful Forward Fold

This Wall Pilates gem is perfect for caressing your hamstrings, lower back, and calves. Here's how to immerse yourself in it:

- Begin by standing with a friendly wall, your feet whispering hip-distance secrets.

- With hands at shoulder elevation on the wall, saunter your feet back, aligning your body in a poised diagonal - imagine you're an elegant plank from crown to heels.

- With an exhale, unfurl forward from your hips. Picture it as a gentle bow to your audience. As you dive, your hands glide down the wall, halting when your muscles sing the sweet tune of a stretch.

- Relish this for a breath-filled 15-30 seconds, then gracefully arise.

- Adapt & Conquer: Find your perfect stretch by flirting with the space between you and the wall. A soft knee bend can be your secret ingredient if hamstrings play hard to get.

The Quaint Quad Stretch

An ode to the thighs, this stretch speaks directly to the front leg heroes.

- Start by standing, serenading the wall, feet again sharing hip-distance tales.

- Your left hand flirts with the wall, while your right foot tries to whisper to your rear.

- Catch that sneaky ankle with your right hand, gently pulling it closer to your buttocks.

- Revel in the thigh's melody for 15-30 seconds, then waltz to the other leg.

- The Ballerina's Tip: Stand tall, with your chest proud and shoulder blades kissing. A forward hip push can amplify the stretch. However, a chat with a healthcare maven is wise if your knees have tales of their own.

The Serene Shoulder Stretch

Unwind those shoulders and upper back, releasing any lingering tales of tension.

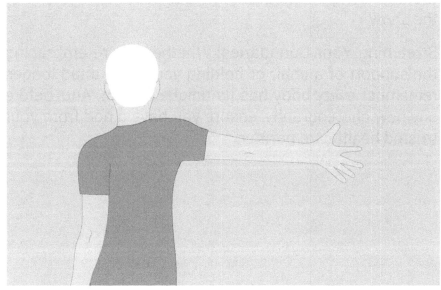

- Standing face-to-face with the wall, gift it your extended right hand.

- Dance into a gentle left twist, perhaps using your left hand for a wall tango.

- Bask in the embrace for 10-15 seconds, unwinding the tales of the right shoulder. Then, switch to the other side's story.

- Safety's Whisper: Shoulders should float like a gentle breeze, and if past injuries lurk, a healthcare whisperer's advice is golden.

Crafting Your Perfect Wind Down:

Alignment Elegance: The beauty is in the details. Inhale the calm, exhale the rush. Your dance should be slow, like the final song of the evening. Your posture? The star of the show.

Stretching Your Boundaries: Whether you're embracing the support of a chair or holding your pose a tad longer, remember every body has its unique rhythm. And, before any new choreography, ensure you have a nod from your trusted healthcare partner.

Chapter 6

CRAFTING YOUR STANDING
WALL PILATES FLOW

Standing Wall Pilates isn't just an exercise; it's an adaptable dance that molds seamlessly to your rhythm and fitness aspirations. Let's walk through the delightful process of choreographing your very own Wall Pilates sequence.

1. Ignite with a Warm-up: Kick off your Pilates show with a heart-pumping opener. This could be as simple as dancing on the spot, embracing some playful jumping jacks, or finding joy in an on-the-spot jog. This sets the tone and preps your muscles for the main act.

2. Curate Your Moves: Immerse yourself in the Standing Wall Pilates library. Choose a harmonious mix of balance-enhancing moves, strength builders, and flexibility flourishes. A balanced cocktail of 8-10 exercises, with the core being the star, can be your sweet spot.

3. Fine-Tune the Reps: Like setting the tempo for a song, decide on your repetition count. If you're just stepping onto the Pilates stage, 8-10 reps sound just about

right. But if you've been around the block and crave intensity, jazz it up to 12-15 reps.

4. Set the Clock: How long do you want your Wall Pilates escapade to last? 20-30 minutes is a splendid curtain-raiser, but feel free to extend or truncate based on your zeal and the time you've got.

5. Graceful Goodbye with a Cool Down: After the standing ovation, gift your body a soothing encore. A few minutes of stretches are like a lullaby for your muscles, ensuring you wake up sans the soreness.

Crafting Your Masterpiece – Pro Tips

- Tailor-made Just for You: Root your routine in what you need. Got wobbly ankles? Focus there. Dreaming of a dancer's flexibility? Add those stretches in.

- Keep It Fresh: A new week deserves a fresh setlist. Redefine your routine periodically to challenge your muscles and keep the excitement alive.

- Balance is Beautiful: Wall Pilates isn't just about that sculpted look; it's also about stability. With every routine, fortify your balance game. After all, a sturdy stance is the real MVP in preventing falls.

- Converse with Your Body: In this Pilates dialogue, your body always gets the final say. If it whispers discomfort, tweak the move. No storyline is worth an injury.

- Seek a Guide: If you're in search of a bespoke Pilates story, rope in an expert. A certified Pilates personal trainer can craft a script that's as unique as you.

Sample routines for different ability levels

Beginner Routines

1. Wall Squats - 10 repetitions
   Single Leg Stand - 10-15 seconds each leg
   Shoulder Stretch - 10 repetitions
   Quad Stretch - 10 repetitions
   Cool-down: Standing Hamstring Stretch - 10 repetitions each leg

2. Wall Press - 10 repetitions
   Lateral Leg Lift - 10 repetitions each leg
   Heel-to-Toe Walk - 10 repetitions
   Shoulder Stretch - 10 repetitions
   Cool-down: Standing Chest Stretch - 10 repetitions each side

3. Wall Plank - 10-15 seconds
   Forward Fold - 10 repetitions
   Single Leg Stand with Leg Lift - 10-15 seconds each leg
   Quad Stretch - 10 repetitions
   Cool-down: Standing Tricep Stretch - 10 repetitions each arm

4. Wall Roll-Down - 10 repetitions
   Lateral Arm Lift - 10 repetitions each arm
   Heel-to-Toe Walk - 10 repetitions
   Shoulder Stretch - 10 repetitions
   Cool-down: Standing Quadricep Stretch - 10 repetitions each leg

5. Wall Squats - 10 repetitions
   Single Leg Stand - 10-15 seconds each leg

Lateral Leg Lift - 10 repetitions each leg
Shoulder Stretch - 10 repetitions
Cool-down: Standing Calf Stretch - 10 repetitions
each leg

Intermediate Routines

1. Wall Squats with Leg Lift - 10 repetitions each leg
   Wall Plank with Leg Lift - 10 repetitions each leg
   Lateral Leg Lift with Knee Bend - 10 repetitions each
   leg
   Shoulder Stretch with Side Bend - 10 repetitions each
   side
   Cool-down: Seated Spinal Twist - 10 repetitions each
   side

2. Wall Press with Arm Reach - 10 repetitions each arm
   Wall Plank with Leg Extension - 10 repetitions each
   leg
   Lateral Leg Lift with Arm Reach - 10 repetitions each
   arm/leg
   Forward Fold with Arm Circles - 10 repetitions
   Cool-down: Seated Hamstring Stretch - 10 repetitions
   each leg

3. Wall Roll-Down with Knee Tuck - 10 repetitions
   Wall Plank with Knee Tuck - 10 repetitions each leg
   Lateral Arm Lift with Knee Lift - 10 repetitions each
   side
   Quad Stretch with Arm Reach - 10 repetitions each
   leg
   Cool-down: Seated Hip Stretch - 10 repetitions each
   leg

4. Wall Squats with Heel Lift - 10 repetitions
   Wall Plank with Arm Reach - 10 repetitions each arm
   Lateral Leg Lift with Knee Tuck - 10 repetitions each leg
   Shoulder Stretch with Arm Circles - 10 repetitions each arm
   Cool-down: Seated Butterfly Stretch - 10 repetitions

5. Wall Press with Knee Tuck - 10 repetitions each leg
   Wall Plank with Leg Circles - 10 repetitions each leg
   Lateral Arm Lift with Leg Lift - 10 repetitions each side
   Forward Fold with Twist - 10 repetitions each side
   Cool-down: Seated Inner Thigh Stretch - 10 repetitions each leg

Advanced Routines

1. Wall Push-Ups - 10 reps
   Wall Plank with Leg Lift - 10 reps (each leg)
   Wall Squat - 10 reps
   Lateral Leg Lift - 10 reps (each leg)
   Single Leg Stand - 30 seconds (each leg)
   Wall Bridge - 10 reps

2. Wall Push-Ups - 15 reps
   Wall Plank with Arm Reach - 10 reps (each arm)
   Wall Squat with Leg Extension - 10 reps (each leg)
   Wall Side Plank - 30 seconds (each side)
   Single Leg Stand with Hip Abduction - 30 seconds (each leg)
   Wall Roll-Down - 10 reps

3. Wall Push-Ups with Knee Tuck - 10 reps (each leg)

Wall Plank with Leg Kick - 10 reps (each leg)
Wall Squat with Calf Raise - 10 reps
Wall Arabesque - 10 reps (each leg)
Single Leg Stand with Knee Flexion - 30 seconds
(each leg)
Wall Lunge - 10 reps (each leg)

4. Wall Push-Ups with Triceps Extension - 10 reps
Wall Plank with Arm and Leg Lift - 10 reps (each side)
Wall Squat with Leg Swing - 10 reps (each leg)
Wall Jumping Jacks - 20 reps
Single Leg Stand with Toe Tap - 30 seconds (each
leg)
Wall Side Lunge - 10 reps (each leg)

5. Wall Push-Ups with Shoulder Taps - 10 reps
Wall Plank with Knee to Opposite Elbow - 10 reps
(each leg)
Wall Squat with Twist - 10 reps (each side)
Wall Knee Drive - 10 reps (each leg)
Single Leg Stand with Knee Extension - 30 seconds
(each leg)
Wall Mountain Climbers - 20 reps

In the vibrant world of Standing Wall Pilates, it's all about staying in the groove. Dive into your routine with dedication, and you'll soon dance with enhanced strength, impeccable balance, and a revitalized zest for fitness. Keep that rhythm, and the magic unfolds!

Chapter 7

ALL YOUR QUESTIONS ANSWERED

Standing Wall Pilates 101

Stepping into the Standing Wall Pilates scene can be a game-changer for seniors craving enhanced strength, impeccable balance, and enviable flexibility. Got questions? You're not alone. Here's a crisp run-down of the top queries on everyone's lips:

Q: Is Standing Wall Pilates a safe bet for seniors?

A: Absolutely! It's tailor-made with seniors in mind. Just give your doc a heads up before you dive in. They can suggest tweaks to make sure you're moving in sync with your body's rhythm.

Q: Any special gear for this?

A: Just a trusty wall. That's your dance partner in this Pilates journey.

Q: I've heard it can boost balance. True?

A: Bang on! Many Standing Wall Pilates moves challenge you to play with weight distribution, jazzing up your balance game.

Q: How often should I groove with Standing Wall Pilates?

A: While every body dances to its own beat, aiming for a solid 2-3 sessions a week should set you on a path to enhanced strength and balance.

Q: Back pain woes. Can this help?

A: You bet! By toning the spine's support squad and refining your posture, Standing Wall Pilates can be a balm for backaches.

Q: What if I'm not quite Fred Astaire on my feet?

A: No worries! This Pilates routine is all about personalization. Seek advice from a pro to ensure you're getting the moves right for your unique groove.

Q: What if a move feels a tad off?

A: Always honor your body's cues. If something feels amiss, pause, and perhaps reconnect with a certified guide for insights.

Q: How long's the dance?

A: Typically, a Standing Wall Pilates session waltzes between 10-30 minutes. But remember, it's your stage. Adjust as you see fit.

Final Note: Always be in tune with your body. Reach out for professional advice when in doubt, and adjust moves to make your Pilates dance safe and sprightly!

Chapter 8

WRAPPING IT UP

The Magic of Standing Wall Pilates

Standing Wall Pilates isn't just any exercise; it's a golden ticket for seniors keen on boosting their strength, flexibility, and balance. By partnering with a wall, Pilates becomes inviting for all, regardless of your mobility dance card. A Few Pearls of Wisdom

Dive in at your pace. Begin with moves that resonate with your current groove and build up the tempo. The mantra? Form and finesse over speed. This ensures you squeeze out every drop of goodness from each move, keeping injuries at bay.

While passion is commendable, remember, it's cool to tap the brakes. Listen to your body, take those breather moments, and always have a chat with a health guru before embarking on a new fitness journey, especially if you've had a stumble or two in the past.

Your Next Steps

Hungry for more Standing Wall Pilates? You're in luck. The world's your oyster, with options aplenty. Maybe join a spirited class at the community hub, or deep dive into the digital realm for some sizzling tutorials. And if you're craving that personal touch, many Pilates maestros offer bespoke sessions tailored just for you.

In Closing

Make Standing Wall Pilates your fitness BFF, and the rewards are manifold. Feel the surge in strength, the grace in flexibility, and strut with newfound balance. Stay the course, and the transformation isn't just physical but touches the soul, ushering in a vibrant, zestful phase of life. Cheers to a brighter, active tomorrow!

Book 3

Seated Wall Pilates for Seniors

Chapter 1

DIVE INTO SEATED WALL PILATES FOR SENIORS

Aging gracefully isn't just about keeping the spirit alive; it's about empowering the body too. While the dance of time has its charm, ensuring that our bodies move and groove becomes paramount. Enter Seated Wall Pilates, the unsung hero for vibrant seniors.

Seated Wall Pilates Unveiled

Traditional Pilates got a comfy makeover and birthed Seated Wall Pilates, tailor-made for the dynamic senior community. If mobility has been playing hard to get or balance feels like a tightrope walk, this is your golden ticket. Picture this: All exercises unfold while you're comfortably seated, with a trusty wall by your side. The essence? Maximum gains, minimal risks.

Perks of the Pilates Chair

Seated Wall Pilates is more than just a workout; it's a wellness potion. It's like gifting your muscles strength and your joints the gift of youth, making wobbles a thing of the past. If creaky joints or posture woes have been stealing your thunder, consider them addressed. But the magic isn't just physical; dive deeper into its rhythmic breaths and feel the stress melt, sharpening the mind and soul.

Your Pilates Toolbox

Ready to embark on this exhilarating journey? Your checklist is simple: A sturdy chair (your throne!) and a faithful wall. If you're itching to spice things up, consider adding hand weights or resistance bands to the mix. They're like the cherry on the Pilates sundae, elevating your game as you progress.

Your Journey Ahead

This guide is more than just words; it's a compass to the world of Seated Wall Pilates. From setting up your Pilates haven, mastering the moves with flair, to adapting to your rhythm, we've got your back. Whether you're just dipping your toes or have been dancing with fitness for a while, every page here promises insights and inspiration. So gear up, because a redefined, vivacious you awaits!

Chapter 2

The Right Start: Warm-Up Exercises

Diving into any exercise routine without a proper warm-up is like setting off on a road trip without checking the oil. Especially as we mature, prepping our muscles becomes paramount. In this chapter, we illuminate the art of warming up for Seated Wall Pilates, ensuring you start off on the right foot—quite literally!

Seated March Magic

A blend of rhythm and focus, the Seated March rejuvenates your hip flexors, quads, and core. Here's how to march to your own beat:

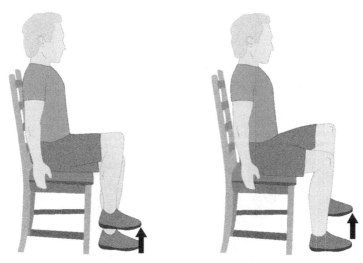

1. Commandeer a sturdy chair and sit with pride, feet firmly grounded, shoulder-width apart.

2. Grip your thighs or the chair's sides for some balance boost.

3. Elevate your right knee as if reaching for the sky, but keep those toes kissing the floor.

4. Bask in this momentary elevation.

5. Gently lower, then march forth with the left.

6. The mantra? Lift, hold, lower, switch. Give it a good 30-60 seconds of gusto.

As you sashay through, envision a rod keeping your back

straight, activate your core, and banish any bouncing.

Shoulder Roll: The Stress-Buster

Untangle those knots of tension with the soothing Shoulder Rolls. Here's your guide to a relaxed upper body:

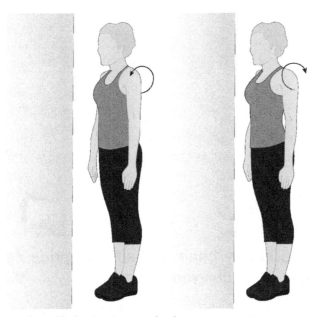

1. Sit tall, feet grounded.

2. Breathe in deeply, rolling your shoulders forward, down, then up towards your ears.

3. Exhale and let them sink back down.

Treat each roll as a mini-massage. Do this for 30-60 seconds and pepper your day with this move to melt away tension.

Ankle Circles: Dance of the Feet

Dip your toes into the Ankle Circles to keep them spry and agile.

1. While seated, extend one leg, letting it hover.

2. Start drawing circles in the air with your toes—clockwise and then counter. A good 10-15 spins each way.

3. Return to earth and repeat with your other foot.

Grace is key. Your circles can be small ballet twirls or wide waltz turns, depending on your comfort.

Golden Rules for a Stellar Warm-Up

- Posture Perfection: Imagine a string pulling you from the top of your head. Stand tall, keep those shoulders relaxed, and let your chest shine.

- Core Connect: Think of your core as your body's control center. Engage it for balance and support.

- Quality Over Quantity: Slow, steady, and controlled. It's a warm-up, not a race.

- Listen to Your Body: If something feels off, halt. Seek guidance if discomfort persists.

Customize to Your Cadence

Everyone's dance of life has a unique rhythm. Here's how to adjust:

- Seated March: Can't lift too high? No problem. Tap your toes in rhythm.

- Shoulder Rolls: Tight shoulders? Small, gentle rolls are your jam.

- Ankle Circles: Lifts not your thing? Keep feet grounded and let those ankles waltz.

Kickstarting your Seated Wall Pilates journey with these warm-ups ensures a safer, more enjoyable workout ahead. Ready, set, glow!

Chapter 3

CORE BOOSTERS FOR THE GOLDEN YEARS

Empower your golden years with Seated Wall Pilates, a fantastic regimen to invigorate those core muscles. Why focus on the core? Well, your core - encompassing the abs, back, and pelvic floor muscles - acts like your body's control center. Keeping it strong not only ensures better posture and balance but wards off back issues and fall risks, concerns that often shadow our senior years.

Let's dive into some game-changing exercises.

Seated Spinal Twist

Give a modern twist to the classic Pilates spinal exercise, designed just for seated wall enthusiasts:

1. Sit poised against the wall, feet grounded.

2. With your right hand on your left knee and the left touching the wall behind at shoulder height, inhale deeply, elongating your spine.

3. Exhale, twisting leftwards. Use your wall hand to deepen the twist.

4. Breathe, hold, feel the stretch.

5. Untwist, inhaling back to the starting point.

6. Time to switch! Now, left hand to right knee and right to the wall.

Not just a spine mobilizer, this move doubles as a core strengthener and a fantastic chest and shoulder stretch.

Seated Cat/Cow

Elevate spinal flexibility with this gem:

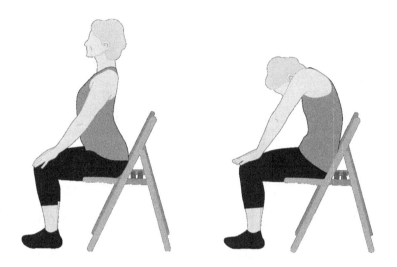

1. Sit tall, feet planted, hands rested on thighs.

2. Inhale, arching into the Cow – shoulders back, chest proud.

3. Exhale, curling into the Cat – chin to chest, spine rounded.

4. Flow between these poses, keeping spine movements fluid.

Tailor this to your comfort level – limit the spinal curve if needed or even try it standing, using a wall for hand support. Regularly indulging in the Cat/Cow dance can vastly enhance posture and free up spine tension.

Seated Leg Lifts

Time to jazz up those quads and hips!

1. Sitting tall, face the wall, hands on it for support.

2. Breathe in, and on exhale, lift a leg forward, keeping it level with the ground, toes poised.

3. Hold briefly, then lower on your next inhale.

4. Swap legs and repeat.

Eager for an upgrade? Slide on some ankle weights or grip a small pilates ball between your ankles. And remember, posture is key: chest up, shoulders easy, core lit.

Golden Rules to Stay Injury-Free

- Always sit tall, keeping shoulders easy and chest buoyant.

- Ignite your core, imagining your navel pulling inwards.

- Value each movement's quality over speed or number.

- Pain is not gain here. If something feels off, pause and consider professional advice.

Modifications for Every Body

We're all unique, so let's respect that:

- Seated Spinal Twist: Challenge with the twist? Just grip your chair's sides and glance over a shoulder.

- Seated Cat/Cow: If the 'Cat' curve feels off, simply emphasize the 'Cow', gazing upwards.

- Seated Leg Lifts: If a full lift feels too much, try an in-place foot march.

Woven into your Seated Wall Pilates routine, these exercises promise a fortified core, an upright posture, and a decreased fall risk. Here's to a stronger, balanced, and more vibrant you!

Chapter 4

Boosting Hip Mobility

Hip mobility isn't just about flexibility; it's the cornerstone of balance, stability, and everyday movement, especially for seniors. In this enlightening chapter, we'll dive deep into Seated Wall Pilates exercises that prioritize hip dynamism, coupled with benefits and adaptable versions for various capability levels.

Seated Hip Circles: A Whirlwind for Your Hips

How-to:

1. Assume a proud sitting posture with both feet grounded.

2. Rest your hands on your knees and take a deep inhale, lifting your spine.

3. As you exhale, let your hips dance in clockwise circles.

4. After 30-60 seconds, switch and groove counter-clockwise.

5. Remember: The dance is in the hips. Keep the upper body gracefully still.

Tip: If there's a hitch in your hip circle or any discomfort, make smaller circles or take a breather. Prioritize comfort.

Seated Figure-Four Stretch: Shape Up Your Hips

How-to:

1. Sit tall and anchor your feet flat.

2. Form a "figure-four" with your legs by placing your right ankle over your left knee.

3. Gently press on your right knee with both hands, deepening the stretch.

4. After 10-15 seconds of this sweet stretch, switch to the other side.

Tip: Ensure you're not slouching or leaning. Always sit like you're wearing a crown. And if your knees protest, modify by gently pressing your knee to the side with your foot still on the floor.

Seated Hip Flexor Stretch: Dive Deep into Flexibility

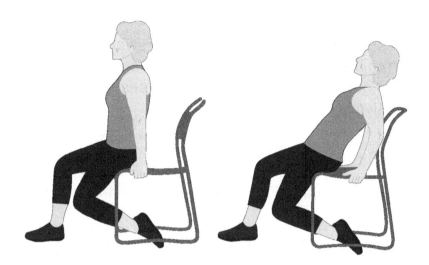

How-to:

1. Begin in a tall seated stance, feet grounded.

2. Glide to the edge of your chair until you're almost taking off.

3. With elegance, move your right foot back, resting it on the chair, toes pointing downward.

4. Inhale, imagining a string pulling your spine upwards. Exhale, press your hips forward, embracing the stretch in your right hip area.

5. Luxuriate in this stretch for several breaths, then switch.

Tip: Stand tall in your sitting. If balance challenges you, a yoga strap or towel can offer a helping hand. Aim for 20-30 seconds per stretch for a profound relaxation experience.

Hip Hip Hooray! The Benefits

Seniors, rejoice! Hip dynamism reaps rewards. From poise and stability to a dwindled risk of trips and stumbles, and ease in mundane tasks, these exercises sprinkle magic into daily life.

Tailored to You: Modifications

Every body is unique, and Seated Wall Pilates celebrates that:

- Seated Hip Circles: If full circles pose a challenge, sway your hips side-to-side or rock them front and back.

- Seated Figure-Four Stretch: If the figure-four formation feels tricky, press your knee gently to the side with your foot rooted.

- Seated Hip Flexor Stretch: If a straight leg is a tall order, slide your foot forward, keeping a bend in the knee.

Here's to a hipper, happier you with Seated Wall Pilates!

Chapter 5

ELEVATING SHOULDER MOBILITY

Shoulders are often the unsung heroes of our daily life, playing a pivotal role in everything from a heartwarming hug to reaching that top-shelf spice. Let's celebrate them! For our senior community, nimble shoulders mean fewer aches, standout posture, and greater ease in day-to-day tasks. Dive into these Seated Wall Pilates exercises tailored to elevate shoulder flexibility and dynamism.

Shoulder Blade Squeeze: Embrace Your Inner Power

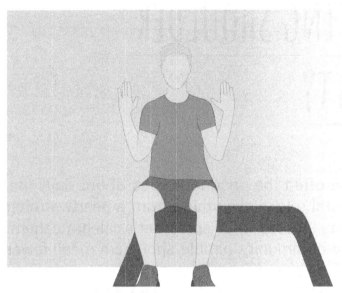

How-to:

1. Sit regally with your back kissing the wall, feet firmly planted.

2. Relax your arms, letting them dangle freely at your sides, and give them a gentle shake to release any built-up stress.

3. Breathe in deeply and imagine hugging a giant tree with your shoulder blades, drawing them down and inward.

4. Hold this warm embrace for a few moments, exhale and let go.

5. Dive back into the squeeze several times.

Pro Tip: This squeeze is like giving your back a mini massage, melting away stiffness often found in seniors. Don't have a wall? No worries! The beauty of this exercise is its adaptability.

Arm Circles: Soar Like an Eagle

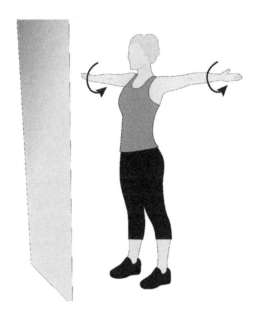

How-to:

1. Sit up tall, feet grounded, arms resting peacefully at your sides.

2. Inhale, lifting your arms sideways and skywards, reaching for the stars.

3. On the exhale, let your arms circle backward and descend like a gentle waterfall.

4. Breathe in again, and now guide your arms forward and up, picturing a soaring bird.

5. Exhale, letting them cascade forward and down, completing the circle.

Pro Tip: Think fluidity. This isn't a race. For an easier version, opt for smaller or slower circles.

Wall Angels: Let Your Shoulders Dance

How-to:

1. Sit tall, back caressing the wall, feet anchored.

2. Keep your arms at your sides, elbows fashioning a right angle.

3. Inhale and elevate your arms to shoulder level, palms greeting the world.

4. Glide your arms up the wall as if crafting a snow angel. Remember, keep those shoulders relaxed and grounded.

5. Once you've reached the peak, bask in it for a few breaths before descending gracefully.

The Perks of Spry Shoulders

Jazzed-up shoulder mobility gifts seniors with an expansive reach, posture that commands attention, and minimal discomfort. Plus, everyday tasks like snagging that high-up cookie jar become a breeze.

Your Pilates, Your Pace: Modifications

Every body has its unique rhythm. Tailor these exercises to your tune:

- For limited mobility: Opt for a shorter movement range or jazz things up with resistance bands or feather-light weights.

- Nursing a shoulder twinge or injury? Modify to comfort, but always consult a healthcare guru before diving in.

Incorporating these shoulder marvels into your Seated Wall Pilates saga not only rejuvenates shoulder vitality but also paints a broader stroke of holistic health. Always remember: Your body whispers its needs; tuning in ensures both comfort and invigoration.

Chapter 6

The Art of Unwinding with Wall Pilates

So, you've just wrapped up a spirited session of Seated Wall Pilates. Bravo! Now, it's time to treat your body to a serene wind-down, stretching out any lingering tension and grounding your energy for whatever lies ahead. Let's dive into these soothing exercises that transition you from workout vigor to a calm oasis.

Seated Forward Bend: Your Serene Bow

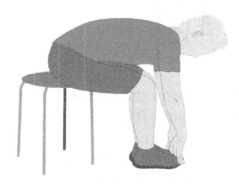

How-to:

1. Sit tall, envisioning a string pulling your spine skyward. Breathe in, embracing this length.

2. As you breathe out, fold forward like the graceful page of a book, letting your fingers whisper towards your toes.

3. Savor this stretch for a moment, then gracefully ascend back to your seated royalty.

Seated Twist: Channel Your Inner Owl

How-to:

1. Sit tall, holding your majestic posture.

2. Lay your left hand on your right knee, while your right hand finds the back of your chair.

3. Inhale, growing taller, and as you exhale, turn right, as if looking over a beautiful shoulder. Switch and give the left its spotlight.

Seated Figure–Four Stretch: A Gentle Embrace

How-to:

1. Sit with grace, placing your right ankle atop your left knee as if crafting the number "4."

2. With hands gently holding your raised leg – right on the knee, left on the ankle – offer a soft push on the knee, deepening your embrace of the stretch.

3. Let it sing for a moment, then switch to serenade the other side.

Shoulder Rolls: Dance of Grace

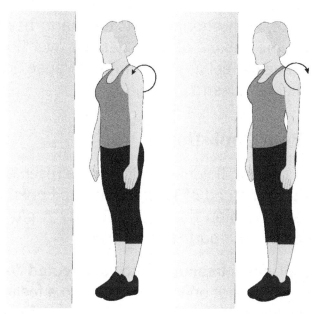

How-to:

1. Sit poised and tall, letting your shoulders rise towards the heavens with an inhale.

2. Exhale, allowing them to flow backward in a graceful dance, descending in completion. After a few rounds, let them waltz in the opposite direction.

Pilates Posture Pearls

It's more than just movements; it's a dance of intention. Hold your elegance, with shoulders at ease and heart forward. Prioritize the finesse of each gesture over how many times you repeat. Feel any discomfort? Pause and chat with a healthcare maestro.

Customizing Your Cool-Down

Every soul has its rhythm. If you're feeling more reserved, reach for your knees instead of toes during the Forward Bend. Need a back cushion during the Twist? A plush pillow or towel can be your partner in comfort.

Weaving these cool-down treasures into your Seated Wall Pilates tapestry ensures not only safety but also a feeling of renewed tranquility and zest. Bask in the glow of your achievements and feel ready for the world.

Chapter 7

CRAFTING YOUR SEATED WALL

PILATES SYMPHONY

Delve into Seated Wall Pilates, a fantastic passport to flexibility, strength, and that ever-so-desired mobility. Designing a symphony tailored to your aspirations ensures you maximize your Pilates voyage. Let's orchestrate your perfect routine, step by step.

Lay Down the First Notes: The Warm-Up

Every great routine kicks off with a gentle prelude. Warm-ups pave the way, making your body receptive to the Pilates magic. They amplify blood circulation, kindle your core temperature, and reduce the chances of an unwanted encore—injury.

- Gentle Stretches: Think of mellow neck, shoulder, and hamstring stretches.

- Shoulder Rolls: Visualize your shoulders dancing in forward and backward circles, limbering up for the main event.

- Ankle Circles: Offer your ankles a twirl, clockwise and

counter, prepping them for the ballet to come.

Warm-ups should be the soft serenades, not the thunderous climaxes. Think of it as setting the tone, not finishing the concert. Breathe, be present, and pave the way for what's next.

The Heart of the Routine: Core Exercises

The core, your body's maestro, sets the tempo. Exercises like seated twists, leg lifts, and pelvic tilts play pivotal roles in enhancing posture, stability, and that swivel in your hips. Consider diversifying your core exercises and occasionally jazzing things up with resistance bands or wee weights. Prioritize elegance of form over vigorous repetitions.

Celebrate Hip and Shoulder Mobility

Hips and shoulders, the unsung heroes, ensure our daily sonatas go uninterrupted. Elements like hip circles, figure-four stretches, arm circles, seated wall angels, and hip flexor stretches weave seamlessly into this Pilates melody, promoting agility and versatility. Adapt exercises to resonate with your rhythm and make sure your form sings the right tune.

Concluding Crescendo: The Cool-Down

End on a gentle lullaby. Let the cool-down be your body's loving encore—a chance to wind down and avoid the aftermath of a rigorous routine. Elements like the doorway chest stretch, shoulder blade squeeze, and Wall Angels harmonize beautifully, helping your muscles release and rejuvenate.

When you craft this masterpiece, remember to harmonize with your body's feedback and rhythm. Every great composition evolves, and so will yours. With that in mind, here are a few sample routines to guide different virtuosos in their Pilates journey...

Beginner Level

Beginner Routine 1:

1. Warm-up: Ankle circles (10 reps each side), Shoulder rolls (10 reps), Seated Cat/Cow (5 reps)

2. Core exercises: Seated spinal twist (5 reps each side), Seated leg lifts (10 reps each side), Pelvic tilts (10 reps)

3. Hip and shoulder mobility exercises: Seated hip circles (10 reps each side), Arm circles (10 reps each direction)

4. Cool-down: Doorway chest stretch (hold for 30 seconds), Seated forward fold (hold for 30 seconds), Shoulder blade squeezes (10 reps)

Beginner Routine 2:

1. Warm-up: Neck rolls (10 reps each direction), Shoulder shrugs (10 reps), Seated Cat/Cow (5 reps)

2. Core exercises: Seated twists (5 reps each side), Seated leg lifts (10 reps each side), Pelvic tilts (10 reps)

3. Hip and shoulder mobility exercises: Figure-four stretch (hold for 30 seconds each side), Wall Angels

(10 reps), Arm circles (10 reps each direction)

4. Cool-down: Doorway chest stretch (hold for 30 seconds), Seated forward fold (hold for 30 seconds), Shoulder blade squeezes (10 reps)

Beginner Routine 3:

1. Warm-up: Ankle circles (10 reps each side), Shoulder rolls (10 reps), Seated Cat/Cow (5 reps)

2. Core exercises: Seated spinal twist (5 reps each side), Seated leg lifts (10 reps each side), Pelvic tilts (10 reps)

3. Hip and shoulder mobility exercises: Seated hip flexor stretch (hold for 30 seconds each side), Arm circles (10 reps each direction), Shoulder blade squeezes (10 reps)

4. Cool-down: Doorway chest stretch (hold for 30 seconds), Seated forward fold (hold for 30 seconds), Neck stretches (hold for 30 seconds each side)

Beginner Routine 4:

1. Warm-up: Neck rolls (10 reps each direction), Shoulder shrugs (10 reps), Seated Cat/Cow (5 reps)

2. Core exercises: Seated twists (5 reps each side), Seated leg lifts (10 reps each side), Pelvic tilts (10 reps)

3. Hip and shoulder mobility exercises: Figure-four stretch (hold for 30 seconds each side), Wall Angels (10 reps), Arm circles (10 reps each direction)

4. Cool-down: Doorway chest stretch (hold for 30 seconds), Seated forward fold (hold for 30 seconds), Shoulder blade squeezes (10 reps)

Beginner Routine 5:

1. Warm-up: Ankle circles (10 reps each side), Shoulder rolls (10 reps), Seated Cat/Cow (5 reps)

2. Core exercises: Seated spinal twist (5 reps each side), Seated leg lifts (10 reps each side), Pelvic tilts (10 reps)

3. Hip and shoulder mobility exercises: Seated hip circles (10 reps each side), Arm circles (10 reps each direction), Wall Angels (10 reps)

4. Cool-down: Doorway chest stretch (hold for 30 seconds), Seated forward fold (hold for 30 seconds), Neck stretches (hold for 30 seconds each side)

Intermediate Level

Intermediate Routine 1:

1. Warm-up: Ankle circles (10 each side), Shoulder rolls (10 each side), Seated twist (10 each side)

2. Core exercises: Pelvic tilt (10 reps), Seated leg lifts (10 each side), Seated knee taps (10 each side)

3. Hip and shoulder mobility exercises: Hip circles (10 each side), Seated figure-four stretch (10 each side), Arm circles (10 each direction)

4. Cool-down: Doorway chest stretch (10 seconds each side), Shoulder blade squeeze (10 reps), Wall Angels (10 reps)

Intermediate Routine 2:

1. Warm-up: Ankle circles (10 each side), Shoulder rolls (10 each side), Seated twist (10 each side)

2. Core exercises: Seated toe taps (10 each side), Seated scissors (10 each side), Seated spinal twist (10 each side)

3. Hip and shoulder mobility exercises: Seated hip flexor stretch (10 each side), Shoulder shrugs (10 reps), Wall angels (10 reps)

4. Cool-down: Doorway chest stretch (10 seconds each side), Seated forward fold (10 seconds), Seated side stretch (10 seconds each side)

Intermediate Routine 3:

1. Warm-up: Ankle circles (10 each side), Shoulder rolls (10 each side), Seated twist (10 each side)

2. Core exercises: Pelvic tilt (10 reps), Seated leg lifts (10 each side), Seated double knee taps (10 reps)

3. Hip and shoulder mobility exercises: Hip circles (10 each side), Seated figure-four stretch (10 each side), Arm circles (10 each direction)

4. Cool-down: Doorway chest stretch (10 seconds each side), Shoulder blade squeeze (10 reps), Seated forward fold (10 seconds)

Intermediate Routine 4:

1. Warm-up: Ankle circles (10 each side), Shoulder rolls (10 each side), Seated twist (10 each side)

2. Core exercises: Seated toe taps (10 each side), Seated scissors (10 each side), Seated spinal twist (10 each side)

3. Hip and shoulder mobility exercises: Seated hip flexor stretch (10 each side), Shoulder shrugs (10 reps), Arm circles (10 each direction)

4. Cool-down: Doorway chest stretch (10 seconds each side), Seated forward fold (10 seconds), Seated side stretch (10 seconds each side)

Intermediate Routine 5:

1. Warm-up: Ankle circles (10 each side), Shoulder rolls (10 each side), Seated twist (10 each side)

2. Core exercises: Pelvic tilt (10 reps), Seated leg lifts (10 each side), Seated knee taps (10 each side)

3. Hip and shoulder mobility exercises: Seated hip circles (10 each side), Seated figure-four stretch (10 each side), Shoulder blade squeeze (10 reps)

4. Cool-down: Doorway chest stretch (10 seconds each side), Wall angels (10 reps), Seated forward fold (10 seconds)

Note: Remember to adjust the number of reps and the difficulty of the exercises based on your individual needs and abilities. Never ignore your body's signals to halt if you experience any pain or discomfort.

Advanced Level

Advanced Routine 1:

1. Warm-up: Seated shoulder rolls - 10 reps forward, 10 reps backward

2. Core exercise: Seated twists with leg lifts - 10 reps each side

3. Hip mobility exercise: Seated hip circles - 10 reps each side

4. Shoulder mobility exercise: Wall Angels - 10 reps

5. Core exercise: Seated leg lifts with double arm circles - 10 reps each side

6. Cool-down: Doorway chest stretch - hold for 30 seconds each side

Advanced Routine 2:

1. Warm-up: Ankle circles - 10 reps each side

2. Core exercise: Seated pelvic tilts - 10 reps

3. Hip mobility exercise: Seated figure-four stretch - 10 reps each side

4. Shoulder mobility exercise: Arm circles with resistance band - 10 reps each direction

5. Core exercise: Seated leg lifts with overhead press - 10 reps each side

6. Cool-down: Seated forward fold - hold for 30 seconds

Advanced Routine 3:

1. Warm-up: Seated neck stretches - 10 reps each side

2. Core exercise: Seated crunches with oblique twist - 10 reps each side

3. Hip mobility exercise: Seated hip flexor stretch - 10 reps each side

4. Shoulder mobility exercise: Seated wall slides - 10 reps

5. Core exercise: Seated leg lifts with shoulder press - 10 reps each side

6. Cool-down: Seated side stretch - hold for 30 seconds each side

Advanced Routine 4:

1. Warm-up: Seated arm swings - 10 reps each side

2. Core exercise: Seated bicycle crunches - 10 reps each side

3. Hip mobility exercise: Seated leg swings - 10 reps each side

4. Shoulder mobility exercise: Seated resistance band pull-aparts - 10 reps

5. Core exercise: Seated leg lifts with side plank - 10 reps each side

6. Cool-down: Seated chest opener - hold for 30 seconds

Advanced Routine 5:

1. Warm-up: Seated shoulder stretches - 10 reps each side

2. Core exercise: Seated plank with knee drives - 10 reps each side

3. Hip mobility exercise: Seated fire hydrants - 10 reps each side

4. Shoulder mobility exercise: Seated reverse fly with resistance band - 10 reps

5. Core exercise: Seated leg lifts with Russian twist - 10 reps each side

6. Cool-down: Seated spinal twist - hold for 30 seconds each side

Chapter 8

Your Queries Answered

Navigating Seated Wall Pilates

Stepping into the world of Seated Wall Pilates can be like opening the first pages of an exciting new book, especially for seniors. Let's demystify this captivating journey with answers to the questions often pondered by curious souls:

Q: Is Seated Wall Pilates a senior-friendly zone?

A: Absolutely! Seated Wall Pilates is tailored to be a gentle embrace for seniors, focusing on low-impact movements that can be personalized for each individual. But hey, a chat with your healthcare advisor before diving in? Always a stellar move.

Q: Ready to start! But what gear do I gather?

A: Keep it simple! Secure a sturdy chair and a wall, and you're set. For those seeking a touch more coziness, a yoga mat can be a soft landing, but it's entirely up to you.

Q: How often should I dip into the Seated Wall Pilates universe?

A: Like any good recipe, it's all about your taste! Aiming for two to three times a week is a wonderful place to start, but always dance to your own rhythm.

Q: Got some back aches. Can Seated Wall Pilates be my remedy?

A: Many have sung praises about how Seated Wall Pilates has bolstered their core and refined their posture, often easing those pesky back troubles. But remember, if your back has a story of its own, consult with a healthcare expert first.

Q: If I need a tweak in the routine for my pace, how do I go about it?

A: Flexibility's the game! Seated Wall Pilates is like a buffet of options. Introduce props like pillows or resistance bands for that added zest or simplicity. Remember, you're the maestro of your journey. Tune it to your comfort.

Q: Can Seated Wall Pilates be my balance buddy?

A: Definitely! It's crafted to reinforce your core, amplifying balance and poise. If balancing acts have been a tad challenging, it's a smart move to consult with a professional to ensure your moves are on point.

Remember, each query unraveled is a step closer to

embracing the magic of Seated Wall Pilates. For our vibrant seniors, it promises a dance of strength, flexibility, and holistic well-being.

Chapter 9

WRAPPING UP THE MAGIC OF SEATED WALL PILATES

Dive into the heart of Seated Wall Pilates and what do you find? A treasure trove perfect for seniors craving strength, flexibility, and equilibrium. This transformative exercise, masterfully blending classic Pilates principles with the stability of a wall, brings the gift of a low-impact workout right to your door.

Journeying through Seated Wall Pilates? Remember, your body speaks – and it pays to listen. As days turn into weeks and months, you might feel the call to up the tempo or perhaps fine-tune your flow, adapting to your evolving vitality and health.

The golden ticket to Pilates prowess? Steady dedication. Slot Seated Wall Pilates into your day-to-day, whether you've snatched a quick moment of calm or carved out a whole hour. There's a universe of exercises waiting, tailored to your aspirations and needs.

Embarking on Your Next Chapter: Nurturing Your Passion

Hungry for more? Dive into local Pilates circles or scout for digital gems — videos, tutorials, and more. A certified Pilates maestro or a seasoned physical therapist can guide you, ensuring each move resonates with safety and efficacy.

Feeling adventurous? Delve into chair yoga's gentle embrace. Designed with a chair's grace and perfect for seniors juggling mobility or balance quirks, it's a worthy companion to Seated Wall Pilates. For a touch of inspiration, Helen Stone's "Chair Yoga for Seniors" is a must-read. Balancing Seated Wall Pilates with chair yoga? You're on a path, lit with vitality and zest, stretching into the horizon.

You can get it by scanning the following QR Code:

Keep in mind, there's no age limit to kickstart a fitness journey. Even minor shifts in your routine can significantly uplift your health and vitality. Keep moving, stay motivated, and don't hesitate to seek guidance from a professional if needed.

Book 4

WALL PILATES FOR SENIORS USING PROPS

Chapter 1

Spicing Up Wall Pilates: The Magic of Props

Welcome to the world of props in Wall Pilates for seniors, a game-changer for adding zest, depth, and dynamism to your workouts. Ever thought of amplifying the challenge or cradling yourself with more support? Props like resistance bands, balls, and blocks aren't just tools—they're your Pilates pals, designed to adapt workouts to your vibe and amplify results.

Dive in as we unveil how props can revolutionize Wall Pilates for seniors. You'll discover:

- Essential props to kickstart your journey

- Pro tips for weaving props into your routines

Sprinkle Some Prop Magic: Why It Matters

Flex Those Muscles: Boosted Flexibility

Props, be it a strap or a simple towel, can be transformative. They extend your reach during stretches and anchor them longer. The result? Enhanced flexibility across the hips, shoulders, and spine. Ever heard of foam rollers? These gems are perfect for melting away muscle tension and amplifying mobility.

Stability Galore: Enhanced Balance

Props don't just challenge; they champion stability. A stability ball might seem playful, but it's a powerhouse for exercises like leg lifts and pelvic tilts, awakening core muscles. Resistance bands? They're not just stretchy ribbons; they ensure you stay aligned, solid, and grounded.

Say No to Strain: Gentle on Joints

Let props be the cushion to your joints. Imagine a comfy pad during kneeling exercises, easing knee pressures, or a block assisting those seated stretches, ensuring your back and hamstrings stay serene.

Pump it Up: Amplified Strength

Add a dash of resistance, and watch your strength soar. Whether it's resistance bands, challenging muscles through their full motion, or weights like dumbbells amplifying exercises such as squats, you're in for power-packed workouts. The golden rule? Start light and let your strength guide the way. Remember, with age might come a natural muscle slowdown, but with resistance training, you've got the magic wand to keep them lively.

Stand Tall: Sculpted Posture

Props are like silent instructors, guiding your body's alignment. A block between the thighs during wall exercises or a ball cradling the lower back can lead to posture that's not just great but grand. The bonus? Efficient breathing, reduced fatigue, and a body that feels in harmony.

Shake it Up: Unleashed Variety

Bid farewell to monotony! With props, every session can feel fresh, exciting, and tailored. Imagine crafting games using props, turning routines into playful challenges, especially for those who might see exercise as daunting. And, for the seniors with unique needs? Props help in molding exercises, ensuring everyone's on board, enjoying, and benefiting.

Embracing props isn't just about adding tools; it's about amplifying the Wall Pilates experience. It's the spice to your routine, promising strength, flexibility, balance, and a fun-filled journey. Ready to elevate your Pilates game? Let's dive deeper!

Essential Props to Elevate Your Wall Pilates Game

Resistance Bands: Flexibility Meets Strength

Think of resistance bands as the multitasking superstars of Wall Pilates. Versatile, portable, and adaptable, these bands come in shades of resistance from feather-light to bring-on-the-challenge heavy. Why settle for a simple bicep curl when you can add that extra zing with a band? From power-packed tricep extensions to deepening hamstring stretches, resistance bands cater to both the stretch-seekers and strength-builders. The best part? Their portability. Roll them up, stash in your bag, and you're set for an anywhere, anytime workout.

Small Ball: Power and Play

The small ball is a secret weapon in Wall Pilates. Slide it between your knees during pelvic tilts or leg lifts, and you've just upped the ante on your core game. Not just strength, this prop is a relaxation guru too. Nestle it between your shoulder blades to kiss upper back tension goodbye. And who said workouts can't be fun? With the small ball, every exercise can feel like playful Pilates.

Yoga Blocks: The Ultimate Pilates Support System

Consider yoga blocks as your trusty sidekicks, ready to offer support, challenge, or a mix of both. Tight hamstrings? A block has your back, making forward bends a breeze. Want to intensify that leg lift? Place a block underfoot and feel the difference. From foam to cork, these blocks cater to every body type, ensuring your Wall Pilates session is both safe and efficient.

Hand Weights: Up the Ante

Hand weights are your passport to a world of intensified

Wall Pilates. Add them to exercises, and you're sculpting muscles with every move. But remember, start small, focus on form, and let your body guide the way. Got arthritis or joint concerns? Best to chat with a healthcare guru before diving in. And if traditional weights aren't handy, DIY with water bottles or canned goods.

Stay Tuned: The Pilates Playbook

The chapters ahead are a goldmine of step-by-step prop action tailored for seniors. From the basics to the advanced, we've got it all mapped out for every fitness aficionado. Let's jump in!

Chapter 2

Dynamic Warm-Ups with Props

Prop up your warm-up! Here's your ticket to a prop-driven warm-up: Resistance Band Shoulder Rolls:

Resistance Band Shoulder Rolls:

- Target: Shoulders, neck, and upper back.

- Execution: Sit tall on a chair. Holding a resistance band at shoulder height, roll your shoulders in big, juicy circles. 8-10 reps forward, then reverse.

- Tip: Go for controlled, fluid movements. Adjust band resistance as you build strength.

Ball Bridge

- Target: Glutes, hamstrings, lower back.

- Execution: Lie back on a mat, knees bent. Squeeze a small Pilates ball between your knees. Lift those hips sky-high! Hold, then lower. 10-12 reps.

- Fun Challenge: Swap the knee ball with a bigger one under your feet. Engage that core!

Block Cat/Cow

- Target: Spine, back, neck.

- Execution: On all fours with hands on a yoga block, arch (cow) and round (cat) your back. Breathe in sync with the motion.

- Tip: The block ensures wrist comfort and optimal alignment. Feel every vertebrae move!

Weighted Arm Circles:

- Target: Shoulders, arms.

- Execution: Stand tall. Weights in hand, extend arms and draw circles in the air. 8-10 reps, then reverse. 2-3 sets.

- Tip: Keep it graceful, not swingy. Start light, then challenge up!

Resistance Band Leg Swings:

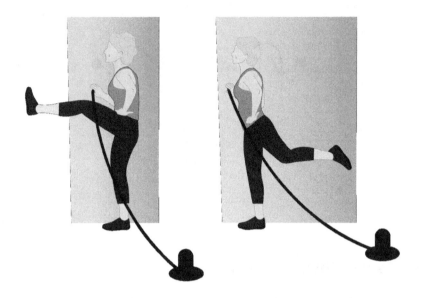

- Target: Hips, legs.

- Execution: Anchor a band, stand sideways to it holding the free end. Swing your leg front and back. 10-15 reps per leg.

- Up the Ante: Anchor the band higher. Feel the hips work!

Remember: Proper form is key. These aren't just exercises; they're your prep for Wall Pilates stardom!

Pro-Tips for Technique & Alignment

- Resistance Bands: Secure well, move with purpose, not haste.

- Small Ball: Neutral spine's the game! The ball squeeze? That's your fame.

- Yoga Blocks: Customize block height. Ensure they enhance, not hinder your might.

- Hand Weights: No swinging. Precision lifting is the thing.

- In Essence: Respect your body. Quality over quantity. Adjust and thrive!

Modifications Tailored to You

Resistance Band Arm Circles:

- Beginner: Light or no band. Smooth circles.

- Intermediate: Medium band. Pick up the pace.

- Advanced: Heavy band, brisker circles.

Small Ball Chest Opener:

- Beginner: Opt for a smaller ball. Or lean against a wall for a gentle stretch.

- Intermediate: Standard ball size, deeper stretch.

- Advanced: Large ball, deep breaths, deeper stretch.

Yoga Block Side Stretch:

- Beginner: Low block or none, with wall support.

- Intermediate: Medium block, hold longer.

- Advanced: Tall block, deep side stretches.

Hand Weight Lateral Raises:

- Beginner: Light weight or none, 90-degree arm bend.

- Intermediate: Moderate weight, straight arms.

- Advanced: Heavy weight, slow and controlled rise.

Your body is unique. Celebrate it. Adjust exercises to suit your rhythm and pace. Happy Wall Pilates!

Chapter 3

ELEVATE YOUR CORE WITH PROPS IN WALL PILATES

Harness the power of props to amplify your core strength in Wall Pilates.

The core isn't just about your abs—it's the powerhouse that connects your upper and lower body. It's a group of muscles wrapping around your torso like a natural corset. Strengthening this area enhances your balance, stability, and overall posture. Props can be a game-changer in targeting these muscles more efficiently.

Why Use Props in Core Training?

- Amplified Strength: Using weights or resistance bands in your routine can intensify the challenge, ensuring your abdominals and back muscles work harder.

- Flexibility Boost: Want to stretch deeper? Balls or blocks can enhance your range of motion, making those core muscles more limber.

- Perfect Your Form: Achieve that flawless technique!

Props can guide you to maintain alignment, maximizing benefits while minimizing risks.

- Tailored Support: Whether you're managing injuries or mobility challenges, tools like blocks or straps can adapt exercises to fit your needs, letting everyone harness the core's power.

So, ready to integrate props into your Wall Pilates journey? They can be the difference between a good workout and a great one!

Tailoring Exercises to Your Level

The beauty of Pilates is its adaptability. Always kick off with the foundational version of an exercise. As you evolve, up the ante. Here's how:

For the Novices:

- Opt for a smaller ball or block. Think of them as your trusty sidekicks.

- Quality over quantity: focus on fewer reps executed perfectly.

- Embrace the power of slow, deliberate movements.

For the Seasoned:

- Challenge yourself with a larger ball or block. It's about pushing boundaries!

- Up the reps. Your core's endurance will thank you.

- Never compromise on form. It's the golden rule.

For the Pilates Pros:

- Introduce resistance bands or hand weights. Feel that burn?

- Test your balance. How about doing exercises on one leg?

- Ramp up the pace! A swift, intense flow keeps those core muscles guessing.

Remember, Wall Pilates is a journey, not a race. Whether you're starting off or pushing your limits, props can be the catalysts propelling you towards your ultimate core goals.

Enhancing Core Workouts with Props in Wall Pilates

Elevate your Wall Pilates sessions by incorporating props into classic core exercises. Not only do these add an interesting twist, but they also boost effectiveness and provide versatility. Let's dive in!

Ball Crunches: A Modern Twist on Classic Crunches

- **Get Ready:** Seat yourself atop a small exercise ball, feet anchored hip-width apart, and knees at a 90-degree angle.

- **The Move:** Roll down until the ball cradles your lower back and hips. Hands behind your head? Check. Elbows flared out? Perfect. Tighten your abs and raise your upper body, breathing out as you rise. Take a pause at the peak and inhale as you descend. Aim for 10-15 reps. And remember—your chin up, elbows wide, and back-to-ball contact are non-negotiables for injury prevention!

Block Planks: Stability Meets Strength

- Get Set: Assume a push-up pose with your hands under your shoulders. Slide yoga blocks under each hand, aligned with your shoulders.

- Engage: Power up your core and glutes. Your body should be a taut line from head to heel. Hang tight for 30-60 seconds. Need an exit? Gently lower your knees, and remove the blocks. With added wrist support from the blocks, this exercise is a godsend for those navigating injuries or seeking better alignment.

Weighted Russian Twists: Amp Up Your Oblique Game

- Setup: Sit with bent knees and feet flat. Hold a weight—dumbbell or medicine ball—at chest height.

- Twist Away: Tilt back slightly, power on those core muscles, and float your shins parallel to the floor. Twist your upper body, guiding the weight towards one hip, then the other. For starters, aim for 8-12 twists each side. To tweak? Drop the weight, plant your feet, or limit the twisting arc. Progress? Heavier weights or more reps!

Resistance Band Woodchops: Emulate the Lumberjack

Start Point: Anchor a resistance band to the wall at chest level. Stand sideways, feet hip-distance, and grab the band.

Chop Time: With arms extended, position the band beside you at hip level. Activate your core and rotate, dragging the band diagonally across and upward, mimicking a wood-chopping motion. After 8-10 reps on one side, switch! Maintain form by ensuring your core's engagement and selecting a band that aligns with your strength level.

Your Body, Your Rules

Prioritize your well-being. Adjust exercises to what feels right. And if in doubt or managing health issues? Always check with your healthcare expert before embarking on new fitness ventures. Happy Pilates-ing!

Chapter 4

Balance & Stability with Props

Upping the Ante

Balance and stability aren't just buzzwords; they're the backbone of daily life and activities. Let's delve into the art of using props to achieve these benefits and modify them to match every fitness level.

Reaping the Rewards of Props in Wall Pilates

Challenge Amplified: Throw in a yoga block or balance disc, and suddenly, your standing exercises aren't as easy. Why? Your muscles are now hustling more to keep you steady, leveling up your strength and coordination. Using resistance bands or small balls can further spotlight those overlooked foot and ankle muscles, which play starring roles in our balance.

Coordination Boost: Think of it as a ballet of muscles. Props make them work in harmony, which is pivotal for activities from squatting with a weighted ball on a balance board to doing push-ups atop a foam roller. Over time, this fine-tuned coordination makes your everyday hustle smoother and counters age-related coordination dips.

Fall-Proofing Your Future: The looming risk of falls becomes less daunting. Thanks to the proprioceptive boost from Wall Pilates with props, you're more in tune with your body's positioning. Using balance balls or foam rollers refines this skill further, enabling you to handle diverse situations. Bonus? As strength and mobility rise, confidence does too, erasing the fear of potential tumbles.

Flexing with Greater Flexibility: Beyond balance, these exercises pack a flexibility punch. Dynamic moves like the single-leg stand with a ball enhance flexibility from toes to fingertips. The added range of motion from exercises, especially with a foam roller, means your body becomes more adaptable and fluid.

Tailoring to Your Tempo: Balance & Stability Progressions

- Rookie Rollout: Begin with the basics. Try the one-legged balance by a wall or with chair support. It's as simple as lifting one foot and timing your balance.

- Intermediate Insights: Up the ante by introducing a balance board or stability ball. Dive into the stability ball plank: elbows on the ball, holding a plank, and embracing the burn for 30-60 seconds.

- Advanced Adventures: Ready to truly test your mettle? Dive into the single-leg squat using a resistance band looped just above your knees. Balance on one leg, squat down, ensuring the band remains taut, and challenge both your strength and stability.

Wrapping Up

Props aren't just for show; they're pivotal players in Wall Pilates. For seniors, they offer a fun twist to regular exercises while magnifying benefits. Whichever stage you're at, there's a prop-enhanced move waiting to boost your balance, stability, and overall fitness journey.

Chapter 5

ELEVATING YOUR BALANCE GAME

Prop up your Wall Pilates routine! Using props not only makes your workout more intriguing but also intensifies the challenge, helping hone balance and stability. Dive into these exercises and watch your form, strength, and balance ascend to new heights.

Block Balance: The Elevator Pose

The Setup: Place a yoga block on the floor. Stand hip-distance apart with the block just ahead.

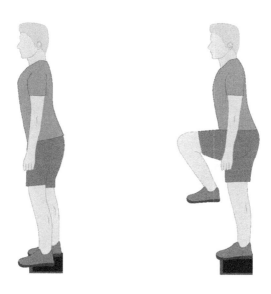

The Flow:

1. Stand on the blocks. Inhale deeply. Exhale and lift one foot, finding your balance.

2. Slightly bend your standing leg. Activate your core to assist in balancing.

3. Feeling stable? Breathe deeply and maintain.

4. Slowly lower your foot with an exhale.

5. Reset with a few breaths and switch sides.

The Pro Tip: Struggling? Begin with a lower prop, like a stout book or even balance on flat ground. With persistence, you'll soon be holding this pose longer, potentially introducing advanced moves like eye-closure or weight transitions.

Wall Squat with a Stability Ball: Thigh Toner Deluxe

The Setup: Align with a wall. Wedge a stability ball between your lower back and the wall, feet shoulder-width apart, slightly away from the wall.

The Flow:

1. Slowly bend your knees, sinking down, ensuring contact between your back, the ball, and the wall.

2. Aim for thighs parallel to the floor.

3. Hold briefly, focusing on form: weight in heels, knees above ankles.

4. Propel yourself back to the beginning with heel power.

5. Aim for 10-15 reps, or as many as pristine form permits.

The Pro Tip: Modify by tweaking your stance or squat depth. Add some spice by clutching a weight or using a resistance band.

Resistance Band Side Step: The Hipster Move

The Setup: Stand evenly with a resistance band looped around your ankles.

The Flow:

1. Step right, stretching the band.
2. Realign with your left foot meeting the right.
3. Step left. Right foot follows.
4. Sidestep for 10-12 reps each way.

The Pro Tip: Engage your core, straighten your back, and keep knees aligned with toes. Adjust band resistance to match your comfort and challenge levels.

Why Props Are a Flexibility Game-Changer

Boosted Stretches: Yoga blocks and straps, for instance, amplify your stretches, honing in on flexibility and movement range.

Body Insights: Props enhance self-awareness. Recognizing your body's boundaries lets you refine your stretching technique, safeguarding against potential injuries.

Comfort and Ease: Props like bolsters and blankets ensure comfort, allowing even those with injuries or limited mobility to find their stretch.

Variety is The Spice of Life: Bored with the usual? Props introduce novel challenges, keeping your routine fresh and stimulating.

Wall Pilates Flexibility Exercises with Props

Resistance Band Hamstring Stretch

This targets the muscles at the back of your thigh.

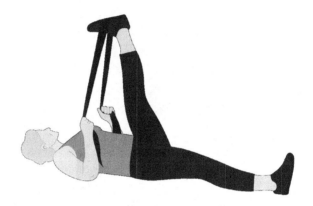

1. Lie down with legs outstretched and loop a resistance band around one foot.

2. With a straight back, pull the band, feeling the hamstring stretch. For added intensity, flex that foot.

3. Switch feet and repeat.

Tip: For a variation, sit on a chair and raise one foot using the band for the same stretch.

Block Triangle Pose

Drawing inspiration from yoga, this exercise leverages a block for a deeper stretch.

1. With a block in one hand, stand facing the wall.

2. Step the opposite foot back and turn it 90 degrees.

3. Extend the hand holding the block to the floor beside your foot, stretching the other hand up.

4. Feel the stretch along the side and switch sides.

Hand Weight Lateral Arm Raises

Tone and stretch your upper body using hand weights.

1. Stand with a weight in each hand.

2. Elevate your arms to the side, stopping at shoulder height.

3. After a brief pause, lower them.

4. For adaptability, you can perform this seated, or alter the weight.

Yoga Block Quad Stretch

Relieve those tight quads and hip flexors.

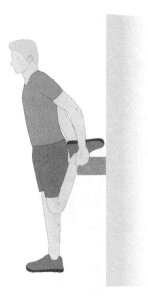

1. With a block in hand, back towards the wall, raising one foot behind and pressing it against a wall-bound block.

2. Lean in for the quad stretch. Switch and repeat.

Resistance Band Shoulder Opener

A savior for tight shoulders and upper back.

1. Holding a band, extend it behind your head.

2. Pull your elbows forward, feeling the stretch, then return to start.

Prop-Driven Adaptability

- Beginners: Start simple. Props like yoga blocks or straps can modify stretches, making them more achievable.

- Intermediate: Venture deeper. Props can intensify your stretch while emphasizing alignment.

- Advanced: Push boundaries, but remember—pain is not gain. Stay mindful to prevent overextension.

In essence, Wall Pilates with props is like adding a secret sauce to your flexibility journey. It's about transforming routine stretches into an engaging experience that pays dividends in flexibility, strength, and mindfulness. Remember, it's not about how far you stretch, but how deeply you connect with your body.

Chapter 6

PROPS-ENHANCED COOL-DOWN EXERCISES

After pushing your limits with Wall Pilates, treat your muscles to a well-deserved cool-down. These exercises, designed specifically for seniors, incorporate props like foam rollers, yoga blocks, and resistance bands to enhance the stretches and ensure your body feels rejuvenated and ready for your next session. Let's dive in:

Foam Roller Upper Back Stretch

Release tightness in your upper back and shoulders with this rejuvenating move.

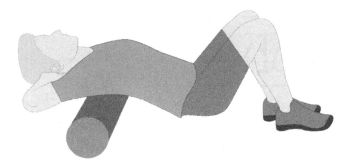

1. Sit down, extend your legs, and position the foam roller horizontally, right under your shoulder blades.

2. Fold your arms or put your hands behind your neck.

3. Gently roll over the foam roller, pausing briefly on knots or tight spots.

4. Keep this up for 1-2 minutes, ensuring your head and neck remain neutral. Adjust the foam roller's position for desired intensity or use your arms for additional support.

Yoga Block Chest Stretch

Counteract the effects of daily hunching and improve your posture with this simple yet effective stretch.

1. Grip a yoga block so its long sides face front and back.

2. Position the block behind you, right at the base of your shoulder blades.

3. Leaning back, adjust your feet and ensure the block aligns vertically between the blades.

4. Deeply inhale, and on the exhale, push your chest forward while pulling the shoulder blades down.

5. After 30 seconds to a minute, gently ease out of the stretch.

Resistance Band Quad Stretch:

This variation intensifies the conventional quad stretch, focusing on flexibility and injury prevention.

1. Stand with feet apart and loop a resistance band's end around your left foot, holding the other end with the same hand.

2. Bend the left knee, moving your heel to your backside, and stabilize with your right leg.

3. With both hands, elevate the band, drawing the heel closer. Ensure both thighs stay parallel and breathe deeply for 15-30 seconds.

4. Gently release and swap sides. Be cautious and always prioritize comfort over intensity.

Wall Supported Pigeon Pose

A blend of tradition and innovation, this stretch targets your hip flexors, glutes, and lower back.

1. Face the wall, extend your hands, and step back to form a diagonal angle with your body.

2. Lift your right knee, placing your ankle on the left thigh above the knee, and flex the right foot.

3. Ease into the stretch by lowering your hips, focusing on a straight spine and relaxed shoulders.

4. Engage for 5-10 breaths, feeling the stretch's essence in your right hip region.

Block Supported Forward Fold:

This Wall Pilates gem elongates the hamstrings, lower back, and spine.

1. Face the wall, distance your feet, and lean onto a yoga block at the wall's base.

2. Inhale and, while exhaling, bend forward, aligning your head with the spine.

3. Rest on the block and let your arms relax for 30 seconds to a minute. Adjust with a different block size or folded towel based on your flexibility.

Essential Alignment & Technique Tips

- Always prioritize comfort. If something feels off, modify it.

- Maintain rhythmic breathing, using each exhale to sink deeper into the stretch.

- Aim for an extended spine and relaxed shoulders to optimize posture.

- Props, like yoga blocks and foam rollers, can intensify or soften a stretch based on their placement.

- Visualize the muscles stretching and releasing tension.

Tailoring for All Abilities

Adjustments ensure everyone reaps the benefits. For instance:

- Foam Roller Upper Back Release: Opt for a softer roller or towel. Try rolling one side at a time for more focus.

- Yoga Block Chest Opener: A smaller block or towel can reduce intensity. Adjust your distance from the wall.

- Resistance Band Quad Enhancer: Use a wall or chair for balance or try a lighter band.

- Block Supported Forward Fold: Slight knee bends cater to tight hamstrings. Adjust prop height to match your flexibility.

Always remember, it's not about how deep you go into a stretch, but how you feel while doing it. Adapt, enjoy, and embrace the journey of Wall Pilates for seniors!

Chapter 7

CRAFTING YOUR PERSONALIZED PROP ROUTINE

When you throw props into the mix, it elevates the experience, tailoring it to your unique body needs. Here's your guide to making Wall Pilates with props work for you.

1. Set Clear Intentions: What are you aiming for? Whether it's enhancing balance, boosting flexibility, building strength, or achieving holistic fitness, defining your goals is step one.

2. Prop It Up: Select from props like foam rollers, yoga blocks, resistance bands, stability balls, or hand weights based on your goals. Ensure they're in tip-top shape before using them.

3. Get That Heart Pumping: Begin with 5-10 minutes of easy cardio. Think about things like spot jogging or a brisk walk in place. This not only warms you up but sets the mood for the workout ahead.

4. Curate Your Moves: Handpick exercises that target varied muscle groups. Remember, it's about getting

a wholesome workout, so don't forget to incorporate moves that utilize your chosen props.

5. Flow with Purpose: Organize your moves in a sequence that feels natural and logical. For instance, transition from balance-centric exercises to strength builders, culminating in flexibility-enhancing stretches.

6. Wind Down: Cap off your session with a serene cool-down. Spend a good 5-10 minutes stretching and perhaps using the foam roller, ensuring your muscles are relaxed and rejuvenated.

Golden Rules for a Tailored Routine

- Progress Over Perfection: Start simple. As you build confidence, you can ratchet up the intensity and complexity.

- Balance is Key: Integrate exercises that zoom in on areas you feel need some extra attention. This ensures a holistic workout.

- Breathers are Essential: Your body appreciates those little rest moments between exercises. They're not just breaks but rejuvenation periods.

- Spice it Up: Every now and then, toss in a new exercise or switch up your props. Variety keeps it fresh and challenging!

- Stay Attuned: Your body speaks. Always. So, listen to its cues and fine-tune your routine, ensuring it's always aligned with how you feel.

Crafting a Wall Pilates routine with props is like painting

on a canvas. There's no one right way. Trust yourself, enjoy the process, and most importantly, have fun moving!

Sample routines for different ability levels

Beginner Routines:

Routine 1:

1. Wall Squat with a Stability Ball - 10 reps

2. Foam Roller Upper Back Stretch - 1 minute

3. Yoga Block Quad Stretch - 30 seconds per side

4. Resistance Band Shoulder Opener - 10 reps

5. Block Triangle Pose - 30 seconds per side

6. Yoga Block Chest Stretch - 30 seconds

Routine 2:

1. Wall Push-Up - 10 reps

2. Resistance Band Side Step - 10 reps per side

3. Resistance Band Hamstring Stretch - 30 seconds per side

4. Block Supported Forward Fold - 30 seconds

5. Hand Weight Lateral Arm Raises - 10 reps

6. Foam Roller Upper Back Stretch - 1 minute

Routine 3:

1. Wall Sit with a Stability Ball - 30 seconds
2. Resistance Band Bicep Curl - 10 reps
3. Yoga Block Quad Stretch - 30 seconds per side
4. Block Supported Forward Fold - 30 seconds
5. Resistance Band Shoulder Opener - 10 reps
6. Block Triangle Pose - 30 seconds per side

Routine 4:

1. Wall Squat with a Stability Ball - 10 reps
2. Resistance Band Side Step - 10 reps per side
3. Resistance Band Hamstring Stretch - 30 seconds per side
4. Block Supported Forward Fold - 30 seconds
5. Hand Weight Lateral Arm Raises - 10 reps
6. Foam Roller Upper Back Stretch - 1 minute

Routine 5:

1. Wall Push-Up - 10 reps
2. Resistance Band Bicep Curl - 10 reps
3. Yoga Block Quad Stretch - 30 seconds per side
4. Block Supported Forward Fold - 30 seconds

5. Resistance Band Shoulder Opener - 10 reps

6. Block Triangle Pose - 30 seconds per side

Intermediate Routine:

Routine 1:

1. Foam Roller Upper Back Stretch (1-2 minutes)

2. Wall Squat with Stability Ball (10 reps)

3. Resistance Band Side Step (10 reps each side)

4. Yoga Block Chest Stretch (30 seconds to 1 minute)

5. Resistance Band Shoulder Opener (10 reps)

Repeat the sequence 2-3 times.

Routine 2:

1. Block Balance (hold for 30 seconds to 1 minute)

2. Resistance Band Hamstring Stretch (10 reps each side)

3. Hand Weight Lateral Arm Raises (10 reps)

4. Yoga Block Quad Stretch (10 reps each side)

5. Block Supported Forward Fold (hold for 30 seconds to 1 minute)

Repeat the sequence 2-3 times.

Routine 3:

1. Wall Supported Pigeon Pose (hold for 30 seconds to 1 minute each side)

2. Resistance Band Bicep Curl (10 reps)

3. Foam Roller IT Band Stretch (10 reps each side)

4. Block Triangle Pose (hold for 30 seconds to 1 minute each side)

5. Yoga Block Chest Opener (10 reps)

Repeat the sequence 2-3 times.

Routine 4:

1. Foam Roller Upper Back Stretch (1-2 minutes)

2. Wall Squat with Stability Ball and Resistance Band (10 reps)

3. Resistance Band Deadlift (10 reps)

4. Resistance Band Quad Stretch (10 reps each side)

5. Yoga Block Supported Forward Fold (hold for 30 seconds to 1 minute)

Repeat the sequence 2-3 times.

Routine 5:

1. Block Balance with Knee Lift (10 reps each side)

2. Resistance Band Tricep Extension (10 reps)

3. Foam Roller Glute Stretch (10 reps each side)

4. Yoga Block Chest Stretch (30 seconds to 1 minute)

5. Resistance Band Shoulder Opener (10 reps)

Repeat the sequence 2-3 times.

Advanced Routine:

Routine 1:

1. Wall Squat with Stability Ball – 2 sets of 10 reps

2. Resistance Band Side Step – 2 sets of 10 reps

3. Resistance Band Hamstring Stretch – 2 sets of 10 reps

4. Yoga Block Chest Stretch – 2 sets of 10 reps

5. Foam Roller Upper Back Stretch – 2 sets of 10 reps

Routine 2:

1. Hand Weight Lateral Arm Raises – 2 sets of 12 reps

2. Resistance Band Quad Stretch – 2 sets of 10 reps

3. Wall Supported Pigeon Pose – hold for 30 seconds to 1 minute each side

4. Block Triangle Pose – hold for 30 seconds to 1 minute each side

5. Resistance Band Shoulder Opener – 2 sets of 12 reps

Routine 3:

1. Resistance Band Bicep Curls – 3 sets of 10 reps

2. Yoga Block Quad Stretch – hold for 30 seconds to 1 minute each side

3. Wall Plank – hold for 30 seconds to 1 minute

4. Block Supported Forward Fold – hold for 30 seconds to 1 minute

5. Foam Roller IT Band Stretch – hold for 30 seconds to 1 minute each side

Routine 4:

1. Wall Push-Ups – 2 sets of 12 reps

2. Resistance Band Lat Pull-Downs – 2 sets of 12 reps

3. Yoga Block Hip Flexor Stretch – hold for 30 seconds to 1 minute each side

4. Wall Supported Single Leg Bridge – 2 sets of 10 reps each side

5. Foam Roller Lower Back Stretch – hold for 30 seconds to 1 minute

Routine 5:

1. Resistance Band Tricep Extensions – 2 sets of 12 reps

2. Yoga Block Inner Thigh Stretch – hold for 30 seconds

to 1 minute each side

3. Wall Supported Tree Pose – hold for 30 seconds to 1 minute each side

4. Foam Roller Chest Opener – hold for 30 seconds to 1 minute

5. Block Supported Forward Fold with Twist – hold for 30 seconds to 1 minute each side

Chapter 8

WALL PILATES PROPS – UNRAVELING THE MYSTERIES

Dive into the fascinating world of Wall Pilates for seniors, enhanced by props! But wait, questions bubbling up? Perfectly normal. Let's address the most common queries to set your mind at ease:

Q: I've got limited mobility and an old injury. Can Wall Pilates props still be a thing for me?

A: Absolutely! But the golden rule? Touch base with your healthcare expert and a seasoned Pilates guru before leaping. They'll guide you with tweaks or alternate moves to ensure you're in the safe zone.

Q: Fancy props are out of my budget. Any DIY alternatives?

A: You bet! Your home's a treasure trove. Think towels for resistance bands or water bottles instead of hand weights. But if you can, investing in dedicated props can up the ante in support and effectiveness.

Q: What's a good frequency for Wall Pilates with props?

A: While daily physical zing is the key, for Wall Pilates props, aiming for 2-3 times a week hits the sweet spot. And remember, a little R&R between sessions is magic for the muscles.

Q: My balance isn't what it used to be. Can Wall Pilates props help?

A: A resounding yes! It's a balance game-changer, especially for seniors. The added dimension from props like stability balls or resistance bands just amplifies the effects. So, fewer wobbles, more confidence!

Q: Looking to shed some pounds. Is Wall Pilates props my golden ticket?

A: While it's a fantastic tool in the fitness arsenal, it's not a standalone weight loss miracle. Its forte lies in sculpting strength, agility, and balance. But here's the kicker: Building muscle revs up your metabolism, making calorie torching more efficient, even at rest!

Lastly, the mantra? Tune into your body's whispers and, when in doubt, seek expert guidance. With heart and hustle, Wall Pilates with props could be the transformative journey you've been waiting for!

Chapter 9

Final Thoughts & The Road Ahead

Diving into the world of Wall Pilates with props has been quite the journey, hasn't it? For seniors, it's not just another fitness regimen. It's an empowering avenue to reclaim flexibility, enhance motion range, and elevate total body wellness. And the magic wand? Props like resistance bands, yoga blocks, and foam rollers. These handy tools can be real game-changers, tailoring workouts to personal needs, and addressing those pesky challenges like balance woes, joint niggles, or that stubborn muscle rigidity.

Here's the lowdown:

- Technique & Alignment: Let these be your North Star. Props are phenomenal, but they're at their peak when used with impeccable technique.

- Tune In: Your body's whispers are louder than you think. Hear its signals, tweak as needed. And while ambition is admirable, starting slow and ramping up is the secret sauce to genuine progress.

- Beyond Wall Pilates: This is a stellar tool in your fitness kit, but remember, there's a wide world of exercise out there. Before diving headfirst into any regimen, a thumbs-up from your healthcare sage is a must.

- Hungry for More? The digital realm is overflowing with resources – think snazzy videos, step-by-step tutorials, or live-streamed classes. Or if in-person guidance is your jam, scout out local classes or even one-on-one sessions with Pilates maestros.

Embarking on this Wall Pilates journey with props isn't just about the workouts; it's a ticket to a vivacious, spry life. As you stride forward, here's to you – stronger, more flexible, and brimming with vitality!

Book 5

Advanced Wall Pilates for Seniors

Chapter 1

Embarking on a Higher Level

The Advanced Wave of Wall Pilates for Seniors

For seniors who've already dipped their toes into the world of Pilates, brace yourself for a thrilling progression! Advanced Wall Pilates isn't just a sequel; it's a revolutionary evolution of the foundational Pilates you've grown to love. Using the trusty wall and an array of innovative props, this regimen amplifies strength, agility, balance, and your inner zen. Designed for those well-acquainted with basic Pilates ethos, let's delve into the transformative journey this advanced module promises.

The Power Punches of Advanced Wall Pilates

- Balance & Stability Unlocked: Aging might come with its fair share of challenges like muscle weakness and reduced flexibility. Enter Advanced Wall Pilates - think of exercises like the Wall Push-Up with Knee Tuck or the Single Leg Squat. These aren't just workouts; they're your personal trainers for impeccable balance. With consistent practice, even simple tasks like walking or standing become smoother. Plus, enhancing balance drastically cuts down fall risks, a prime concern for seniors, given the CDC's data on injury-induced fatalities in older adults.

- Strength & Flexibility Amplified: Push your boundaries! The advanced variant demands more, fostering both muscle strength and limberness. The wall, alongside the props, emphasizes toning pivotal muscle areas — from legs to core. This paves the way for better posture, minimized back issues, and an easier time with daily chores. Greater flexibility means reduced stiffness and a broader range of motion, propelling you towards an active, independent life.

- Posture Perfected: Aging sometimes stoops the shoulders and curves the spine. Advanced Wall Pilates spotlights muscles pivotal for spine support. The result? An upright stature, improved breathing, and a burst of self-confidence. A proper alignment not only adds aesthetic appeal but also harmonizes weight distribution, ensuring a steady gait and diminished fall risks.

- Mental Wellness Boosted: Here's a perk that's often overlooked — the mental rejuvenation Wall Pilates provides. The regimen isn't merely physical; it's deeply intertwined with breathing patterns and mindfulness, forming a shield against stress and anxiety. Moreover, studies resonate with Pilates being a mood elevator, fighting off depressive symptoms, and elevating overall mental well-being.

- Tailored Just For You: No two seniors are the same. Recognizing this, Advanced Wall Pilates is moldable, fitting perfectly into any senior's life, irrespective of fitness levels. Under a seasoned instructor's eye, you can twist, turn, and tailor exercises, ensuring comfort, safety, and efficiency. Whether it's employing a prop, adjusting the movement arc, or recalibrating resistance levels, there's always a way to make Wall Pilates your own. Personalization, apart from ensuring safety, keeps motivation soaring high.

In essence, Advanced Wall Pilates isn't just about fitness; it's a holistic approach to senior wellness. It's about the thrill of challenging oneself, the joy of movement, and the peace of mindfulness. By embracing this practice, seniors open doors to a life brimming with vitality, independence, and joy. Welcome aboard!

Embarking on Advanced Wall Pilates: A Guide to Get You Started

Transitioning to advanced Wall Pilates is akin to taking your fitness journey up a notch. But like any adventure, the right preparation ensures you reap the maximum benefits without the setbacks. Here's a streamlined guide to pave the way for your Advanced Wall Pilates expedition:

- Medical Green Light: It's paramount to check with your healthcare professional before diving into new fitness waters, especially if you have any existing health quirks. They're the best judge of the exercises suitable for you or if certain tweaks are necessary.

- Strengthen Your Base: Think of Advanced Wall Pilates as building a skyscraper; a robust foundation is non-negotiable. Familiarize yourself with the core Pilates tenets and ensure your core muscles are primed and ready.

- Gear Up with a Warm-Up: Jumpstarting your session without warming up is a rookie mistake. Engage in dynamic stretches like arm windmills or leg pendulums. Alternatively, light cardio, like brisk walking, can also get your blood pumping.

- Props are Your Pals: Some advanced exercises can be a handful. Don't shy away from using props like blocks, straps, or foam rollers. They're not crutches but tools to elevate your exercise precision and safety.

- The Art of Perfect Form: The essence of Wall Pilates, especially the advanced variants, lies in maintaining impeccable form. Prioritize alignment and keep that core engaged. It's your secret sauce to maximizing benefits and sidelining injuries.

- Listen to Your Body's Whispers: Your body is constantly communicating with you. Feeling a tad exhausted or sensing discomfort? Hit the pause button, take a breather, and resume when you're ready.

- Hydration is Key: Imagine working out as revving up your body's engine. To keep it running smoothly, stay amply hydrated pre, during, and post-session. It's your shield against muscle cramps and the dreaded dehydration aftermath.

In the dance of Advanced Wall Pilates, you lead while your

body follows. Stay attuned to its rhythms, know when to push and when to pull back. With these guidelines in your arsenal, you're set to embrace the transformative power of Advanced Wall Pilates. Onward and upward!

Chapter 2

CRANK UP THE HEAT WITH WARM-UPS

Before we plunge into the adrenaline-pumping world of Advanced Wall Pilates, we need to set the stage. Consider these warm-up exercises your backstage prep. They get the blood pumping, loosen up the muscles, and prime you to tackle more advanced moves without a hitch.

Roll Down with Flair: Wall Roll-Downs

Let's give those spines, cores, and shoulders a mini-workout. Your posture will thank you later.

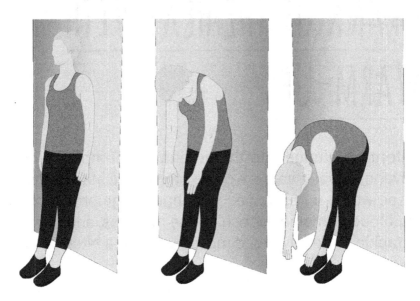

- How-To: Stand flush against the wall. Inhale and elongate your spine. Now exhale, and let's unravel that spine down towards the floor, think of it as peeling away from the wall.

- Spice It Up: Change the foot distance or use a yoga block for a custom fit. Breathe in rhythm to your movements, and visualize each vertebra moving like a string of pearls.

Lower–Body Love: Wall Squats

Tone those quads, hammies, and glutes while engaging your core.

- How-To: With your back against the wall, step forward a bit and squat down until your thighs are parallel to the floor. Keep that back flat against the wall, people!

- Bonus Tip: Keep the knees over those ankles and please, no leaning. Want more oomph? Hold a small weight or medicine ball while you squat.

Lunge Like You Mean It: Wall Lunges

Lunges are the unsung heroes of lower body workouts. Let's bring 'em into the limelight.

- How-To: Facing the wall, take one foot back and lunge. Keep that front knee in check—never let it go past your toes.

- Alignment Alert: Engage that core and keep your weight even on both feet. The wall is your sidekick, not your crutch.

Upper-Body Uplift: Wall Push-Ups

This one's a gem for sprucing up your chest, shoulders, triceps, and yes, even your back.

- How-To: Stand facing the wall, arms straight and palms against the wall. Engage your core and lean in, bend those elbows!

- Breathing 101: Inhale as you go down and exhale as you push away from the wall.

Swinging into Action: Wall Leg Swings

Unlock hip mobility and add zest to your lower extremities.

- How-To: Plant yourself in front of the wall. Shift your weight onto one foot and let the other swing forward and back.

- Pitfall to Avoid: Control is king. Keep your movements smooth to avoid a balance blunder.

Aim for 10-15 reps or 30-60 seconds for each exercise. Trust your body—if you need a breather, take it.

Nailing Technique & Alignment

- Core Commander: Keep those abs engaged; they're your built-in corset.

- Spinal Sense: Imagine a string pulling you upward; let's avoid that Quasimodo look.

- Shoulder Savvy: No shrugging, keep those shoulders down and relaxed.

- Breathwork: Your breath is your internal metronome; keep it steady.

- Pacing: Rome wasn't built in a day. Ease into the new moves and escalate as you get comfy.

- Prop it Up: Use props like bands or blocks to maintain alignment or offer extra support.

- Body Talk: If something feels off, tweak it or take a breather.

Tailoring to Your Tunes: Modifications for You

- Props are Not Faux-Pas: Use blocks, bands, or foam rollers for a customized experience.

- Range Tweaks: New to the Advanced Wall Pilates game? Limit your range or reps.

- Lighten Up: Use lighter weights or bands to ease into the program.

- Balance Buddies: Grab a chair or wall if stability is your Achilles' heel.

- Rest and Revive: It's okay to pause. Your body's telling you something—listen.

Remember, Advanced Wall Pilates is all about progressing safely while keeping things spicy. By staying mindful and embracing these modifications, Wall Pilates becomes a rewarding challenge for seniors at every fitness stratum. Happy Exercising!

Chapter 3

SUPERCHARGE YOUR CORE

So, you're craving that next-level core activation, huh? Welcome to the world of advanced Wall Pilates core work. A well-honed core isn't just for six-packs; it's your body's powerhouse. It's like your internal superhero suit that keeps you steady, upright, and moving with oomph. So, let's unpack these rockstar moves.

Wall Plank: The Ultimate Core Challeng

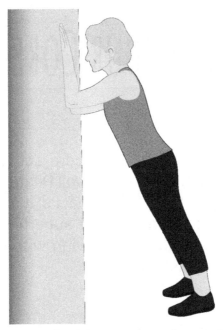

- How-To: Stand with your hands on the wall. Now walk those feet back until you're a human plank. Hold this sizzle for 30 to 60 seconds.

- Elevate It: Keep those hips level—no drooping or hiking up. Feel it's too much? Start with shorter intervals or keep your feet closer to the wall.

Wall Roll-Ups: Curl Like You Mean It

- How-To: Stand facing the wall, arms out, palms down. Curl down one vertebra at a time, till your hands flirt with the wall. Unwind back up.

- Customize Your Curl: If you need to make it simpler, roll down less at first. You can also wedge a foam roller or a yoga block against the wall to assist your roll.

Wall Oblique Twist: Twist Your Way to a Dynamic Core

- How-To: Face the wall with your arms stretched out and palms touching the wall. Now lift your left knee and twist your core, aiming that knee toward your right elbow. Hold, and release. Time to switch sides!

- Your Twist, Your Rules: Not into the big twist? No sweat! Start with a mini-twist and work your way up.

Wall Bridge: Amp Up Those Glutes and Hamstrings

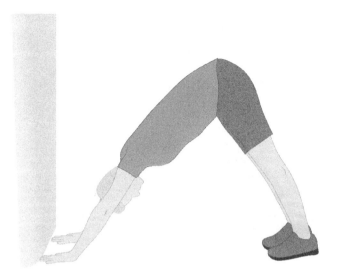

- How-To: Starting in the standing position, walk your hands down the wall till you hit an 'L' shape. Walk those feet back, and push those hips sky-high.

- Bridge Builders: Shorten your hold time or your range if you're just starting out. Need more? Incorporate a resistance band or yoga block to kick up the heat.

Wall Pike: Skyrocket Your Core Strength

- How-To: Stand an arm's length from the wall. Place your palms on it and assume a diagonal plank. Now, lift those hips, make like a mountain, and come back down.

- Performance Tips: Keep your ears between those arms and maintain a straight back. Start with fewer reps and let your core acumen guide you.

Perks of a Turbocharged Core in the Golden Years

- Steady as You Go: Better core strength means less wobbling and tumbling. Translation? Fewer falls.

- Bye-Bye, Back Pain: A robust core can be a lifesaver for your back, offering more support and less strain.

- Flex, Bend, Move: Enjoy a broader range of motion for everything from tying your shoelaces to swinging a golf club.

- Digest This: Believe it or not, a stronger core can even perk up your digestion. Less bloating? Yes, please.

- Breathe Easy: Ever feel like you're short of breath? A stronger core can literally lift your ribcage, giving your lungs more room to expand.

Tailor-Fit Your Core Routine: Make It Yours

1. Bent Knees: If your abs are throwing in the towel or your back's shouting, just bend those knees a bit.

2. Handy Props: A yoga block under your back or a weighted ball in your hands can tweak an exercise from "ugh" to "ahh."

3. Limit the Stretch: If you're less Gumby, more Tin Man, just reduce your range of motion. Little by little, you'll get there.

4. Hold Your Horses: Need a breather? Reduce the holding time for each exercise, then gradually lengthen it as you gain endurance.

Listen, the key here is making Wall Pilates work for you. Modifications aren't cheats; they're your personalized ticket to core glory. So grab your props, flex those abs, and let's get this Wall Pilates party started!

Chapter 4

BALANCE AND STABILITY MASTERCLASS

Why Balance Matters for Seniors

Hey, hotshot! So you're on the prowl for a rock-solid core, but what about your balance and stability? As we move up in years, keeping our equilibrium becomes the name of the game. Welcome to advanced Wall Pilates—a surefire way to supercharge your stability and keep you on your feet.

Advanced Wall Pilates: Balance Boosters

Single Leg Balance: One Leg, No Sweat!

- How-To: Stand close to the wall. Use one hand for a little wall support, lift one leg, and let the balancing act begin.

- Flex-Time: Try 10-30 seconds per leg, then swap.

- Adjust the Dial: If that's tough, dial it down by holding for 5-10 seconds. Need more spice? Toss those hands on your hips or shut those eyes.

Wall Squats with One Leg Raise: Add Flair to Your Squats

- How-To: Get into a squat against the wall. As you rise, lift one leg, bending the knee towards your booty.

- Go Pro: Hold that lifted leg for a couple of seconds before gracefully landing it back down.

- Custom Fit: Wanna ease in? Use a yoga block between your thighs and limit the depth of your squat. Or, grasp a chair for extra support.

Wall Push-Ups with Leg Lift: Push-Up, Level Up

- How-To: Assume a diagonal plank against the wall, lift one leg, then descend into a push-up.

- Balance Hack: Keep that core tight and make sure your weight is evenly spread between both hands and feet.

- Boost It: Feel ready for more? Prolong the push-up position or up the reps.

Wall Plank with Leg Lift: The Plank's Showy Cousin

- How-To: Assume a plank position against the wall. Tighten that core, lift a leg and keep it straight.

- The Fine Print: Keep those hips level and the back from arching.

- Pro-Tip: Start with a knee push-up if a full plank is too much too soon. Build from there.

Wall Lunge with Leg Lift: Lunge & Lift Combo

- How-To: Lunge down, then lift the back foot towards your chest.

- Nail the Technique: Keep that front knee over the ankle and distribute your weight on the front heel.

- Safety First: Use the wall for support, or keep that back foot grounded if balance is a bit wobbly.

Unbeatable Perks of Wall Pilates for Seniors

Fall-Proof Your Life: Navigating life without tripping over your own two feet? Priceless. Advanced Wall Pilates techniques can be your secret weapon against gravity.

Walk with Swagger: A stable you equals a more confident you, and that could mean a world of independence.

Stand Tall, Feel Great: Better balance often spells better posture, saving you from backaches and earning you style points.

Unlock Your Inner Athlete: Even in the senior leagues, stability can take your athletic game to the next level. Who says you can't teach an old dog new tricks?

Make It Yours: Customizable Wall Pilates

1. Use Props: Hold onto a chair or wall for extra support during your exercise.

2. Limit the Lift: Got limited mobility? No worries. Try smaller leg lifts.

3. Short & Sweet: Low stamina? Opt for shorter holds—10-15 seconds works wonders.

4. Two's Company: Start on both feet, then work your way up to one-legged wonders.

5. Sit & Get Fit: Can't stand? Get those seated leg lifts and marches going.

Remember, you've got to make Wall Pilates work for you. So whether you're using props, limiting range of motion, or opting for shorter holds, it's all good. As always, consult with a certified Pilates guru to make sure you're getting the most out of your exercise while staying in your comfort zone. So, let's get you steady on those feet and turn you into a Wall Pilates virtuoso!

Chapter 5

FLEX THOSE MUSCLES— ADVANCED FLEXIBILITY

Why Flexibility Is Your Golden Ticket

Flexibility is a critical player in the senior fitness game, essential for keeping you spry, resilient, and most of all, comfortable in your own skin. Ready to deep-dive into Wall Pilates to ramp up your flexibility? Let's go!

Advanced Wall Pilates: Your Flexibility Toolkit

Wall Roll-Downs: Unwind Like a Pro

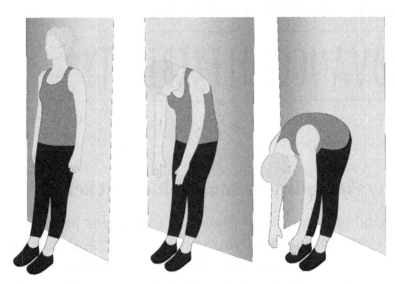

- How-To: Stand against the wall, back straight, feet spread. Inhale deeply, then exhale while rolling down your spine toward the floor. Hello, flexibility!

- Smooth Operator: The key is fluid motion. Think of your spine unrolling one vertebra at a time.

- Mix It Up: Having a hard time touching the floor? Pop a yoga block under your hands. A little bend in the knees also spares your lower back.

Wall Chest Stretch: Open Your Heart

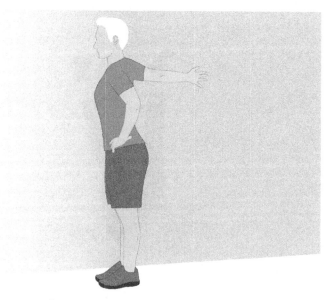

- How-To: Face the wall, arms outstretched. Step back with one foot and lean in to stretch out your chest.

- Feel the Love: Hold that glorious stretch for 15-30 seconds. Inhale, exhale, enjoy!

- You Do You: Shoulder issues? Place your palms lower on the wall. For those wobbly on their feet, widen your stance or grab something stable.

Wall Hamstring Stretch: Loosen Those Guitar Strings

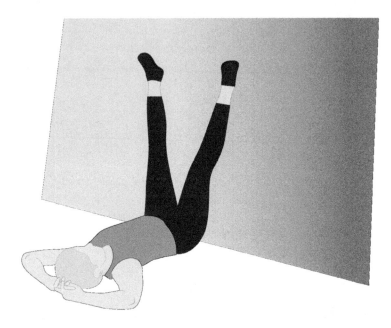

- How-To: Lie on your back, legs up on the wall. Walk your heels down the wall until you feel a stretch, but not to the point of discomfort.

- Walk the Line: Remember, this isn't a leg-straightening contest. The aim is to stretch your hamstrings while respecting your body's limits.

- Raise Your Game: As you get more comfortable, try holding the stretch longer or walking your heels a bit further down the wall.

Wall Hip Stretch: Hip Hip Hooray!

- How-To: Place your hands on the wall, take a step back with one foot, and lunge forward with the other.

- Pro Tip: Hold for 20-30 seconds, then flip sides. And keep that core engaged—no slouching!

- Chair Champs: Mobility issues? Ditch the wall for a chair and follow the same steps for a gentler approach.

Wall Shoulder Stretch: Reach for the Stars

- How-To: Extend arms on the wall and walk your feet back. Lower your chest to the wall and feel the stretch.

- Hold It: A few deep breaths in this position will work wonders.

- Shoulder Savvy: Got shoulder issues? Cut the range of motion or switch to a softer surface like a padded wall.

The Golden Rewards of Flexibility

- Armor Against Injuries: A flexible body is like built-in armor against trips, falls, and muscle strains.

- Move Like Jagger: Stiff joints can seriously cramp your style. Flexibility sets you free.

- Balance Bonanza: Flexibility tunes up your balance by keeping your muscles limber and ready for action.

- Bye-Bye, Pain: Stretching can be your best friend if you're dealing with pain and stiffness, especially from arthritis.

One Size Doesn't Fit All: Modify Your Moves

1. Props Galore: Yoga blocks or straps can bring the stretch to you.

2. Time Crunch: Short on stamina? No worries. Shorten the hold time.

3. Easy Does It: You can dial down the stretch range if your mobility isn't what it used to be.

4. Tender Loving Care: For those with aches or conditions, tailor the stretches to what feels good for you.

Conclusion: Flex Your Way to Wellness

With Advanced Wall Pilates, the path to a more flexible you is literally just a wall away. The beauty of these exercises? They're totally customizable. So, you can tailor each stretch to your comfort level and still snag all the benefits. Whether you're a Pilates novice or a seasoned vet, your flexibility can only go up from here. So let's roll down that wall and stretch it out, shall we?

Chapter 6

CHILL OUT IN STYLE— ADVANCED COOL-DOWN

The Art of Cooling Down

Hey there, fitness enthusiasts! You've powered through those wall Pilates, and you're feeling like a rockstar. Now it's time to cap it off with the perfect cool-down. Why? Because your muscles deserve some TLC after all that hard work. Let's get into some sophisticated, wall-based cool-down exercises to stretch it out and wind down like pros.

Your Go-To Cool-Down Exercises Using the Wall

Wall Shoulder Opener: Unshackle Those Shoulders

- How-To: Stand tall, face the wall, and raise your arms up to say "hi!" Now walk your feet back as you lean in. Feel that stretch across your chest and shoulders?

- Hold It: Let's breathe deeply for 15-30 seconds and savor this feel-good stretch.

- Pro Tips: Too intense? Ease up by moving closer to the wall. If you're chair-bound or less mobile, no worries—you can still join the party from your chair.

Wall Chest Opener: Let Your Heart Sing

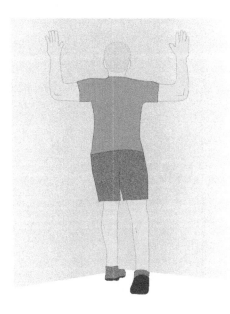

- How-To: Stand square, palms pressed into the wall at shoulder height. Now step back, pressing your palms and stretching your upper body. Ah, freedom!

- Fine-Tuning: Adjust hand height for comfort and depth of stretch.

- Mix It Up: Want to focus on one side? Shift your weight a bit. To lower intensity, step closer to the wall.

Wall Figure Four Stretch: The Hipster Stretch

- How-To: Lean at a 45-degree angle against the wall. Cross your right ankle over your left knee (yes, like a "4"). Feel that hip stretch? Heavenly, right?

- Time It: Hold that fabulous stretch for 30-60 seconds, then switch sides.

- Safety First: Always respect your body's limits. Stop immediately if something doesn't feel right.

Wall Hamstring Stretch: The Leg Whisperer

- How-To: Plant your hands on the wall and step one foot back. Feel the pull along the back of your thigh? You're stretching those hamstrings like a pro.

- Alignment Check: Keep that back straight and knee slightly bent.

- Fine Print: Intensity too much? Try a little knee bend or lower your heel to the floor.

Wall Seated Forward Fold: Sit, Stretch, Smile

- How-To: Sit and extend your legs straight ahead, toes nudging the wall. Walk your hands down the wall until you feel that awesome hamstring stretch.

- Hold and Breathe: 15-30 seconds of deep, blissful breaths here.

- Tailor-Made: Need a lift? Sit on a yoga block. More flexible? Walk those hands further down.

Cool-Down Commandments: Alignment and Technique

- Straight Spine: Always keep your spine straight. We're cooling down, not slouching down.

- Breath Control: Breathing is your best buddy. Deep inhales, slow exhales. Feel the zen.

- Go Slo-Mo: Slow, mindful moves maximize benefits and minimize the risk of pulling something.

Personalizing Your Cool-Down

- Scope Adjustment: Limited mobility? No problem. Simply reduce the range of motion.

- Props Galore: Yoga blocks, pillows—use 'em if you need 'em.

- Quickies: Stamina still catching up? Shorten the holding time for each stretch.

Wrapping It Up

Cooling down is more than a ritual; it's your body's "thank you" note after a strenuous workout. So always listen to your body and tweak these Advanced Wall Pilates cool-downs to fit your unique needs. Whether you're a Pilates newbie or a die-hard fan, ending your session with these cool-down exercises will keep you flexible, centered, and ever-ready for the next workout extravaganza. So go ahead, stretch it out and chill—you've earned it!

Chapter 7

Level Up with Your Advanced Routine

Your Journey to Unbeatable Fitness

Hey there, fitness gurus! Ready to step up your game? Advanced Wall Pilates is your VIP ticket to strength, flexibility, and dynamite balance. Seniors, this chapter's just for you! From laying out the building blocks of an elite Wall Pilates routine to tailor-made tips and sample sessions—consider this your blueprint for next-level fitness.

The Four Pillars of Advanced Wall Pilates

Core Charge-up

Go-To Exercises: Wall Plank, Wall Roll-Ups, Wall Oblique Twists

Your core is your power center. Spice up your session with these ab-ripping wonders, and say hello to core strength!

Balance Bonanza

Go-To Exercises: Single Leg Balance, Wall Squats with One Leg Raise, Wall Push-Ups with Leg Lift

Trust me, you're gonna be as steady as a rock. Nail these exercises and forget the phrase "I've fallen and can't get up!"

Flexy and Flowy

Go-To Exercises: Wall Chest Stretch, Wall Figure Four Stretch, Wall Hamstring Stretch

Think of this as yoga's cool cousin. Get flexy with these moves and kiss stiffness goodbye.

Strength Symphony

Go-To Exercises: Wall Lunges with Leg Lift, Wall Pike, Wall Bridge

Become your own Hercules. These exercises are a muscle-packed fiesta for every part of you.

Crafting Your Advanced Wall Pilates Masterpiece

Find Your North Star

Before diving in, identify your personal fitness dreams. Whether it's core strength, enhancing your balance, or getting more limber, your goals set the stage for your workout saga.

Pick the Peaks

Your Wall Pilates routine should push your limits without going overboard. The golden rule? Go challenging but achievable. The right exercises are ones you can nail with flawless form.

All-Around Athlete

The Wall Pilates playground is vast. Sample everything! Your routine should be a buffet of core, balance, flexibility, and strength exercises. We're talking whole-body tune-up.

Mix and Match

Add zing to your routine with modifications. Whether it's using funky props, dialing down the hold times, or adjusting the range, your workout can be as unique as you are!

The Pre-Party and After-Party

Never underestimate the power of a solid warm-up and cool-down. A couple of minutes of stretching and deep breathing can go a long way. Think of it as setting the stage and then basking in the glory.

Your Wall Pilates, Your Rules

You've got the tools. Now build your Wall Pilates

skyscraper. Make it personal, make it fun, and most importantly, make it yours. Whether you're new to the game or a seasoned pro, a tailored Advanced Wall Pilates routine can ignite your fitness journey and keep those golden years truly golden.

Remember, your Wall Pilates session is your daily act of self-love. So put your back to that wall and let's get rockin'!

5 Sample Routines for Different Ability Levels

Here are some sample routines for different ability levels:

Beginner Level:

Routine 1: Beginner Full-Body

1. Wall Roll-Downs - 10 repetitions

2. Wall Push-Ups - 10 repetitions

3. Wall Squats - 10 repetitions

4. Wall Bridge - 10 repetitions

5. Wall Plank - hold for 30 seconds

6. Wall Chest Opener - hold for 30 seconds

7. Wall Hamstring Stretch - hold for 30 seconds

8. Wall Shoulder Stretch - hold for 30 seconds

9. Wall Seated Forward Fold - hold for 30 seconds

Routine 2: Beginner Core-Focused

1. Wall Roll-Ups - 10 repetitions
2. Wall Plank with Leg Lift - hold for 20 seconds on each side
3. Wall Pike - 10 repetitions
4. Wall Oblique Twist - 10 repetitions on each side
5. Wall Leg Swings - 10 repetitions on each side
6. Wall Hamstring Stretch - hold for 30 seconds
7. Wall Figure Four Stretch - hold for 30 seconds on each side

Routine 3: Beginner Balance and Stability

1. Single Leg Balance - hold for 20 seconds on each side
2. Wall Squats with One Leg Raise - 10 repetitions on each side
3. Wall Push-Ups with Leg Lift - 10 repetitions on each side
4. Wall Plank with Leg Lift - hold for 20 seconds on each side
5. Wall Lunge with Leg Lift - 10 repetitions on each side
6. Wall Hip Stretch - hold for 30 seconds on each side
7. Wall Shoulder Opener - hold for 30 seconds on each side

Routine 4: Beginner Flexibility

1. Wall Roll-Downs - 10 repetions

2. Wall Chest Stretch - hold for 30 seconds

3. Wall Hamstring Stretch - hold for 30 seconds on each side

4. Wall Figure Four Stretch - hold for 30 seconds on each side

5. Wall Seated Forward Fold - hold for 30 seconds

6. Wall Shoulder Stretch - hold for 30 seconds on each side

7. Wall Chest Opener - hold for 30 seconds

Routine 5: Beginner Upper Body

1. Wall Push-Ups - 10 repetitions

2. Wall Chest Opener - hold for 30 seconds

3. Wall Shoulder Stretch - hold for 30 seconds on each side

4. Wall Shoulder Opener - hold for 30 seconds on each side

5. Wall Plank with Leg Lift - hold for 20 seconds on each side

6. Wall Pike - 10 repetitions

7. Wall Chest Stretch - hold for 30 seconds

Intermediate Level

Routine 1: Intermediate Full Body Workout

1. Wall Roll-Ups - 10 reps
2. Wall Squats with One Leg Raise - 10 reps each leg
3. Wall Push-Ups with Leg Lift - 10 reps each leg
4. Wall Pike - 10 reps
5. Wall Chest Stretch - 30 seconds
6. Wall Hamstring Stretch - 30 seconds
7. Wall Shoulder Stretch - 30 seconds
8. Wall Figure Four Stretch - 30 seconds each leg

Routine 2: Intermediate Core and Balance Workout

1. Wall Oblique Twist - 10 reps each side
2. Single Leg Balance - 30 seconds each leg
3. Wall Plank with Leg Lift - 10 reps each leg
4. Wall Lunge with Leg Lift - 10 reps each leg
5. Wall Hamstring Stretch - 30 seconds
6. Wall Chest Opener - 30 seconds
7. Wall Hip Stretch - 30 seconds each leg
8. Wall Shoulder Opener - 30 seconds each side

Routine 3: Intermediate Upper Body Workout

1. Wall Push-Ups - 10 reps
2. Wall Tricep Dips - 10 reps
3. Wall Shoulder Press - 10 reps
4. Wall Chest Stretch - 30 seconds
5. Wall Shoulder Stretch - 30 seconds
6. Wall Chest Opener - 30 seconds
7. Wall Shoulder Opener - 30 seconds each side

Routine 4: Intermediate Lower Body Workout

1. Wall Squats - 10 reps
2. Wall Lunges - 10 reps each leg
3. Wall Bridge - 10 reps
4. Wall Hamstring Stretch - 30 seconds
5. Wall Hip Stretch - 30 seconds each leg
6. Wall Figure Four Stretch - 30 seconds each leg

Routine 5: Intermediate Flexibility and Balance Workout

1. Wall Roll-Downs - 10 reps
2. Wall Seated Forward Fold - 30 seconds
3. Wall Chest Stretch - 30 seconds
4. Single Leg Balance - 30 seconds each leg

5. Wall Hamstring Stretch - 30 seconds

6. Wall Hip Stretch - 30 seconds each leg

7. Wall Shoulder Opener - 30 seconds each side

Advanced Level:

Routine 1: Advanced Core Focus

1. Wall Roll-Ups: 3 sets of 10 reps

2. Wall Oblique Twist: 3 sets of 10 reps each side

3. Wall Pike: 3 sets of 10 reps

4. Wall Plank with Leg Lift: 3 sets of 10 reps each side

5. Wall Bridge: 3 sets of 10 reps

Routine 2: Advanced Balance and Stability

1. Single Leg Balance: 3 sets of 30 seconds each side

2. Wall Squats with One Leg Raise: 3 sets of 10 reps each side

3. Wall Push-Ups with Leg Lift: 3 sets of 10 reps each side

4. Wall Lunge with Leg Lift: 3 sets of 10 reps each side

5. Wall Plank with Leg Lift: 3 sets of 10 reps each side

Routine 3: Advanced Flexibility and Mobility

1. Wall Hamstring Stretch: 3 sets of 30 seconds each side

2. Wall Shoulder Stretch: 3 sets of 30 seconds each side

3. Wall Figure Four Stretch: 3 sets of 30 seconds each side

4. Wall Hip Stretch: 3 sets of 30 seconds each side

5. Wall Seated Forward Fold: 3 sets of 30 seconds

Routine 4: Advanced Full-Body

1. Wall Roll-Ups: 3 sets of 10 reps

2. Wall Squats with One Leg Raise: 3 sets of 10 reps each side

3. Wall Push-Ups with Leg Lift: 3 sets of 10 reps each side

4. Wall Lunge with Leg Lift: 3 sets of 10 reps each side

5. Wall Plank with Leg Lift: 3 sets of 10 reps each side

6. Wall Shoulder Opener: 3 sets of 30 seconds each side

7. Wall Chest Opener: 3 sets of 30 seconds each side

Routine 5: Advanced Cardio and Endurance

1. Wall Burpees: 3 sets of 10 reps

2. Wall Squats with One Leg Raise: 3 sets of 10 reps each side

3. Wall Push-Ups with Leg Lift: 3 sets of 10 reps each side

4. Wall Lunge with Leg Lift: 3 sets of 10 reps each side

5. Wall Plank with Leg Lift: 3 sets of 10 reps each side

6. Wall Mountain Climbers: 3 sets of 10 reps

7. Wall Jumping Jacks: 3 sets of 10 reps

Conclusion

In closing, let's dive into the world of Advanced Wall Pilates, a delightful avenue for seniors to embark on a journey of strength, balance, and flexibility. With a thoughtful blend of core-focused moves, stability-enhancing exercises, flexibility stretches, and strength-building routines, seniors can craft a fitness regimen that caters to their unique goals. This chapter has offered valuable insights and sample routines to help you shape an Advanced Wall Pilates routine that's not only effective but also keeps safety in the spotlight. It's time to embrace the challenge and enjoy the remarkable benefits that await you on this path to a healthier, more vibrant you.

Chapter 8

The Real Deal—FAQs

Your One-Stop Source for All Things Advanced Wall Pilates

Hey there, savvy seniors! Ready to elevate your fitness game but have some burning questions? Don't worry; I've got you covered. Let's dive into the most asked questions about mastering the art of Advanced Wall

Q: Is Advanced Wall Pilates a Safe Bet for Seniors?

A: Great question! First and foremost, always give your healthcare provider a ring before jumping into any new exercise regimen—Advanced Wall Pilates included. But here's the good news: When done correctly, Advanced Wall Pilates is not only safe but a game-changer for improving your strength, flexibility, and balance. Key to this? Team up with a pro instructor and let your body be your guide.

Q: What Could Possibly Go Wrong? Common Concerns Unpacked.

A: Let's keep it real. Whether it's worrying about nailing those complex moves or wondering if Pilates will play nice with your arthritis, we all have our set of concerns. Communication is key! Loop in your instructor about your medical history or specific fears so they can tailor the moves to suit you. Oh, and if life's just too hectic for a regular Pilates rendezvous, remember—consistency trumps intensity.

Q: How Often Should I Be Hitting the Wall?

A: You do you, but a good rule of thumb is aiming for 2-3 sessions per week. Consistency is your best friend when it comes to seeing transformative results.

Q: Need Any Cool Gadgets?

A: Pilates purists, rejoice! All you need is a wall and a mat to get started. But if you're into accessorizing your workout, throw in some yoga blocks or resistance bands. These aren't essential but can amp up the fun and challenge.

Q: How Do I Spot a Wall Pilates Guru?

A: Credentials matter, especially in Pilates land. Search for instructors with a green light from trustworthy organizations like the Pilates Method Alliance. Pro tip: local gyms and community centers often have a lineup of certified instructors who specialize in working with seniors.

Q: Is Advanced Wall Pilates the Answer to My Aches?

A: Look, Pilates is no magic wand, but it's a solid player

in the team sport that is pain management. While it's not a replacement for medical advice or treatment, it can certainly complement your existing pain relief strategies by boosting strength, flexibility, and balance.

Q: When Will I Start Feeling Like Superman or Wonder Woman?

A: Patience, grasshopper! Results can vary, but many find they're more nimble, stronger, and balanced after just a few weeks. The trick? Stick to your routine like glue.

Q: Can I Still Do Advanced Wall Pilates with a Medical Condition?

A: First up, high-five your healthcare provider for personalized advice. That said, Advanced Wall Pilates can often be modified to accommodate various health conditions. A qualified instructor can help you navigate through the moves while keeping it safe and fun.

Conclusion: Your Pilates Adventure Awaits

Hey, it's a jungle out there, but you've got the answers to brave your Advanced Wall Pilates journey. Armed with this FAQ guide, you're ready to make informed choices and, more importantly, have a blast while doing it! So go ahead, give that wall a nudge; it's your new fitness ally.

Chapter 9

Your Next Chapter— Unlocking Your Best Self

The Finish Line is Just the Beginning!

Hey there, you fitness trailblazer! You've made it through the ultimate guide to Advanced Wall Pilates for seniors, and that's worth celebrating. You're now equipped with the ins-and-outs of how Pilates can elevate your game—boosting your strength, balance, and flexibility in ways you might not have even imagined.

Small Steps, Giant Leaps

No shame if you're not yet pulling off Pilates moves like a Cirque du Soleil performer! Remember, every master was once a beginner. Pilates is incredibly versatile and forgiving, adapting to your pace and comfort zone. Keep at it, stay consistent, and soon you'll be pulling off advanced poses that make you feel like a rockstar.

So, What's Next?

Ready to level up? Local classes are a great way to immerse yourself in the Pilates community and get personalized guidance. Virtual classes can also be an excellent way to keep your momentum going, especially if you're all about that at-home comfort. Just a heads-up: get your doc's approval before embarking on any new fitness quests, especially if you've got some medical backstories.

The Bigger Picture

Brace yourself for an awesome revelation: Advanced Wall Pilates isn't just about rocking a stronger core or nailing that balance; it's about unlocking a better you. Picture this—waking up with more energy, tackling your day with newfound confidence, and basically, owning your life like never before. That's the transformative power of Pilates, my friends.

Parting Shots

Your foray into Advanced Wall Pilates is more than a fitness regimen; it's a lifestyle switch that beckons more joy, health, and vitality into your life. Trust this guide to be your trusty sidekick in your ongoing adventure toward a sprightlier, more invincible you.

Until then, keep bending, keep stretching, and most importantly, keep shining!

Book 6

WALL PILATES ROUTINES FOR SENIORS

Chapter 1

Kickstart Your Wall Pilates Adventure!

Welcome to the Wall Pilates Universe

Hey, wellness warriors! Get ready to redefine what "aging gracefully" means to you. Wall Pilates is more than just another exercise—it's a lifeline to reclaiming your strength, flexibility, and balance in a way that's tailor-made for seniors. So, let's delve into routines that are crafted just for you.

Unveiling the Magic of Wall Pilates for Seniors

Let's talk perks—Wall Pilates is more than just a good time; it's a goldmine of benefits for anyone in the golden years. Here's what's in store:

- Power Up: Wall Pilates isn't just a flex-fest; it's your go-to for building that all-important muscle, particularly in the powerhouse zones like your core, arms, and legs.

- Flex to Impress: If you've been missing the good ol' days of bendy youth, Wall Pilates has got your back—

and your hamstrings, and your arms. Prepare for enhanced flexibility and a wider range of motion that makes everyday life a breeze.

- On the Ball: If balance is a game, Wall Pilates makes you the MVP. And let's be real—having better balance is a big win when you're looking to dodge those risky falls.

- Easy on the Knees: Here's the best part for those with creaky joints: Wall Pilates is your low-impact hero, going easy on those knees, hips, and elbows. Whether you've got arthritis or just some general aches and pains, this is your safe zone.

The Golden Rules of Wall Pilates

Ready to rock these routines? Keep these savvy guidelines in your back pocket for a practice that's as safe as it is effective.

- Posture Perfect: Align like a star! Keeping that spine in check and those shoulders relaxed sets you up for a flawless Pilates session.

- The Art of Slow: We're building strength and balance, not racing to a finish line. Make each move a masterpiece by performing it with deliberate, controlled finesse.

- Breathe Easy: You've breathed for decades; now make it count. Inhale through that nose like you're smelling a rose and exhale through the mouth like you're cooling off hot tea. Your breath is your secret weapon for acing these exercises.

- Custom Fit: One size doesn't fit all in Wall Pilates—or in life! That's why there are plenty of tweaks and mods you can make to suit your level, be it beginner-genius or Pilates-prodigy.

So, who's ready to embrace routines that are not just exercises, but also a passport to a more vivacious, agile life? Let's get this wellness party started!

Chapter 2

YOUR WALL PILATES LAUNCHPAD—LET'S DO THIS!

Prepping the Ultimate Pilates Playground

Excited to get your Wall Pilates groove on? First thing's first, let's make sure your space and gear are all set for a killer workout. Trust me, this is like setting the stage for a rock concert—your performance will be so much better!

Your Wall Pilates Toolkit

Nope, you don't need a home gym or fancy gadgets to get started with Wall Pilates. It's all pretty straightforward, but let's run through the essentials:

- Your Trusty Wall: Find a solid, flat wall with enough space to let you bust a move without knocking into anything. This will be your new best workout buddy!

- A Yoga Mat: Grab a yoga mat that doesn't slide around. This is your soft landing and your grip central for hands and feet during poses.

- Towel or Blanket: A little extra cushion for the pushin'

(and pullin', and liftin'). Think of this as your comfort accessory, particularly for exercises that might need a tad more padding.

- H2-Oh Yeah: Your exercise VIP—Very Important Prop. A refillable water bottle to keep you refreshed and hydrated. Bonus? No plastic waste, so you're doing good while feeling good!

Limber Up for Your Wall Pilates Adventure

Wall Wisdom: Your How-To Guide

The wall is not just a space-filler; it's an all-in-one Pilates prop that adds some zesty flavors to your workout recipe. So, let's get the best out of it, shall we?

Wall as Your Alignment Guru:

Who needs a mirror when you've got a wall? For rockstar alignment, make sure your head, shoulders, hips, and heels are aligned like a chart-topping harmony during exercises.

Wall as Your Support Crew:

When you're doing Wall Squats or Wall Push-Ups, the wall becomes your reliable backup singer—keeping you steady and strong.

Wall as Your Resistance Band:

When it's time for Wall Roll-Downs or Wall Leg Lifts, your

wall morphs into your Pilates resistance band, upping the ante on your strength and flexibility.

With these tips in your toolkit and a dollop of enthusiasm, you're all set to make Wall Pilates the hottest ticket in your wellness routine. Ready to break a leg? Metaphorically, of course!

Chapter 3

YOUR FIRST WALL PILATES

PLAYLIST!

Ready to take the plunge into Wall Pilates? Perfect, because we've curated a beginner-friendly Pilates playlist, just for you! And guess what? You don't need to be a pro to jam to these tunes. We've got all the deets on how to personalize each move to your own rockin' rhythm.

Pre-Show Prep: Your Body's Soundcheck

Let's kick things off with a warm-up, your body's very own soundcheck. Keep it simple and effective. March in place like you're the grand marshal of your own parade or glide into some easy, breezy stretches. If you've been tuning into our previous books, you might already have a few go-to warm-up moves. Bring 'em on!

The Wall Pilates Setlist for Newbies

No two Wall Pilates concerts are alike! That's the beauty of it. Here's your beginner's setlist—a collection of hits designed to get you movin' and groovin':

5 sample workout plans for beginners

Routine 1:

1. Wall Squats: 10 reps

2. Wall Push-Ups: 10 reps

3. Wall Roll-Downs: 5 reps

4. Wall Shoulder Stretch: hold for 30 seconds

5. Wall Hamstring Stretch: hold for 30 seconds

6. Wall Chest Stretch: hold for 30 seconds

Routine 2:

1. Wall Lunges: 5 reps per leg

2. Wall Plank: hold for 30 seconds

3. Wall Figure Four Stretch: hold for 30 seconds per leg

4. Wall Chest Opener: hold for 30 seconds

5. Wall Seated Forward Fold: hold for 30 seconds

Routine 3:

1. Wall Push-Ups with Leg Lift: 10 reps per leg

2. Wall Shoulder Opener: hold for 30 seconds

3. Wall Hamstring Stretch: hold for 30 seconds

4. Wall Squats with One Leg Raise: 5 reps per leg

5. Wall Chest Stretch: hold for 30 seconds

Routine 4:

1. Wall Plank with Leg Lift: 10 reps per leg

2. Wall Hamstring Stretch: hold for 30 seconds

3. Wall Shoulder Stretch: hold for 30 seconds

4. Wall Lunge with Leg Lift: 5 reps per leg

5. Wall Chest Opener: hold for 30 seconds

Routine 5:

1. Wall Roll-Downs: 5 reps

2. Wall Squats: 10 reps

3. Wall Push-Ups: 10 reps

4. Wall Figure Four Stretch: hold for 30 seconds per leg

5. Wall Seated Forward Fold: hold for 30 seconds

Hey, don't forget to listen to your body's cues. Think of them as your personal feedback loop. If something doesn't feel right, it's time to hit the remix button and adjust the track—that is, the exercise—until it's your kind of jam.

Customize Your Jam Session

Think of these exercises like songs you can remix. If a move feels like it's on a higher octave than you're used to, modify it to suit your range. You can adjust the distance between you and the wall, or use props like a yoga block to tailor each exercise to your vibe.

So, why wait? Your Wall Pilates stage is set, and it's showtime, baby! Get ready to be the star of your own health and wellness tour.

Not Sure How to Remix?

No worries. When you're unsure how to tweak a move, it's like needing a recommendation for the next hit song. Time to reach out to your go-to Wall Pilates maestro—a certified instructor who knows all the lyrics, er, techniques, for a safe and groovy workout.

Coming Up: The Intermediate Stage

You've got your warm-up down and you're comfortable with the beginner's playlist. What's next? Oh, just you wait! We're cranking up the volume in the next chapter with some Wall Pilates routines for the seasoned groove masters among us—aka the intermediates. So, keep those dancing shoes on; this party is just getting started!

Chapter 4

Level Up Your Game – Intermediate

Hey there, Wall Pilates Rockstar! Kudos for nailing the beginner routines and craving something a little more daring. Welcome to your next adventure: Intermediate Wall Pilates. This chapter unveils a killer lineup of routines custom-crafted for folks like you, who are ready to elevate their game.

Keep the Vibe Safe and Groovy

Before we dive into these hot tracks, let's keep a couple of things in mind. First, safety is still the headliner. No exercise should ever feel like you're crossing into the danger zone. If a move triggers discomfort or, heaven forbid, pain, hit pause and either remix the move or skip to the next track—there's no shame in that game.

Your Pre-Party Checklist: The Warm-Up

Now, you wouldn't start a car without warming it up in

winter, right? Consider your body the same; never skip the warm-up. Get that blood flowing and those joints lubricated. We're talking about more than just tapping your toes here!

Tailor-Made Wall Pilates: Customize Your Jam Session

Find yourself stuck on a tricky verse? Change it up! If Wall Plank with Knee Tucks feels like a tongue twister, ditch the leg lifts. Or if Wall Squats with Arm Reaches are turning into a high note you can't hit, just let go of the arm reaches. The key is to keep the groove going without compromising on your safety or form.

So, are you ready to hit the next stage? Your backstage pass to a fitter, more fabulous you is right around the corner!

5 Sample workout plans for intermediate practitioners

Workout Plan 1:

1. Wall Squats - 10 repetitions
2. Wall Push-Ups - 10 repetitions
3. Wall Roll-Downs - 10 repetitions
4. Wall Plank - hold for 30 seconds
5. Wall Hamstring Stretch - hold for 30 seconds on each side
6. Wall Chest Stretch - hold for 30 seconds on each side

The circuit should be repeated three times.

Workout Plan 2:

1. Wall Lunges with Leg Lift - 10 repetitions on each side
2. Wall Push-Ups with Leg Lift - 10 repetitions on each side
3. Wall Chest Opener - hold for 30 seconds
4. Wall Figure Four Stretch - hold for 30 seconds on each side
5. Wall Shoulder Opener - hold for 30 seconds on each side
6. Wall Seated Forward Fold - hold for 30 seconds

The circuit should be repeated three times.

Workout Plan 3:

1. Wall Single Leg Balance - hold for 30 seconds on each side
2. Wall Push-Ups - 10 repetitions
3. Wall Shoulder Stretch - hold for 30 seconds on each side
4. Wall Hamstring Stretch - hold for 30 seconds on each side
5. Wall Plank with Leg Lift - hold for 30 seconds on each side
6. Wall Chest Stretch - hold for 30 seconds on each side

The circuit should be repeated three times.

Workout Plan 4:

1. Wall Squats with One Leg Raise - 10 repetitions on each side
2. Wall Push-Ups with Leg Lift - 10 repetitions on each side
3. Wall Roll-Downs - 10 repetitions
4. Wall Hip Stretch - hold for 30 seconds on each side
5. Wall Shoulder Stretch - hold for 30 seconds on each side
6. Wall Seated Forward Fold - hold for 30 seconds

The circuit should be repeated three times.

Workout Plan 5:

1. Wall Lunge with Leg Lift - 10 repetitions on each side
2. Wall Push-Ups - 10 repetitions
3. Wall Hamstring Stretch - hold for 30 seconds on each side
4. Wall Chest Opener - hold for 30 seconds on each side
5. Wall Shoulder Opener - hold for 30 seconds on each side
6. Wall Figure Four Stretch - hold for 30 seconds on each side

The circuit should be repeated three times.

Chapter 5

ELEVATE YOUR GAME WITH ADVANCED WALL PILATES ROUTINES

You've crushed the beginner and intermediate levels, and now you're ready for the Wall Pilates major leagues. Kudos to you! Advanced Wall Pilates is the next frontier, and it's designed to take your strength, flexibility, balance, and general wellness to star-studded heights. This is where we merge challenging movements and brain-boosting techniques for a complete mind-body symphony.

Tips to Tailor Your Advanced Moves

Tune into Your Body's Signals

Your body is always communicating with you, so tune in! If something feels off, or you're in the 'ouch' zone instead of the 'ahh' zone, modify or omit that exercise.

Get Creative with Props

Props aren't just for show and tell; they can be game-changers. If a pose feels like a stretch too far, yoga blocks or resistance bands can be your best allies. Think of them as your supporting cast in this Pilates production.

Level Up Wisely

If you're looking for a challenge, by all means, go for it. But remember, Rome wasn't built in a day. Take gradual steps in boosting your workout's intensity and length. Your body will thank you later.

So, get ready to steal the spotlight in your Pilates journey with these advanced routines that turn up the dial on challenge and excitement. Your next chapter in fitness starts here!

5 Sample workout plans for advanced practitioners:

Advanced Wall Pilates Workout A:

1. Wall Plank with Leg Lift (3 sets of 10 reps each side)
2. Wall Roll-Downs (3 sets of 10 reps)
3. Wall Push-Ups with Leg Lift (3 sets of 10 reps each side)
4. Wall Hamstring Stretch (hold for 30 seconds each leg)
5. Wall Shoulder Stretch (hold for 30 seconds each arm)

Advanced Wall Pilates Workout B:

1. Wall Squats with One Leg Raise (3 sets of 10 reps each leg)
2. Wall Lunge with Leg Lift (3 sets of 10 reps each leg)
3. Wall Figure Four Stretch (hold for 30 seconds each leg)
4. Wall Chest Opener (hold for 30 seconds)
5. Wall Shoulder Opener (hold for 30 seconds)

Advanced Wall Pilates Workout C:

1. Wall Push-Ups with Knee Tucks (3 sets of 10 reps)
2. Wall Seated Forward Fold (hold for 30 seconds)
3. Wall Hamstring Stretch with Side Bend (hold for 30 seconds each leg)

4. Wall Hip Stretch (hold for 30 seconds each leg)

5. Wall Chest Stretch (hold for 30 seconds)

Advanced Wall Pilates Workout D:

1. Wall Lunge with Knee Lift (3 sets of 10 reps each leg)

2. Wall Plank with Knee Tucks (3 sets of 10 reps)

3. Wall Roll-Downs with Arm Reach (3 sets of 10 reps)

4. Wall Shoulder Stretch with Side Bend (hold for 30 seconds each arm)

5. Wall Hamstring Stretch with Leg Lift (hold for 30 seconds each leg)

Advanced Wall Pilates Workout E:

1. Wall Squats with Leg Lift (3 sets of 10 reps each leg)

2. Wall Push-Ups with Leg Extension (3 sets of 10 reps)

3. Wall Shoulder Opener with Arm Reach (hold for 30 seconds each arm)

4. Wall Chest Opener with Backbend (hold for 30 seconds)

5. Wall Hip Stretch with Knee Lift (hold for 30 seconds each leg)

Remember to always consult with a healthcare provider before beginning a new exercise routine, especially if you have any medical conditions or concerns.

Chapter 6

Make Wall Pilates Your Own: Personalized Routines for Seniors

The Art of Tailoring Your Practice

You're unique, and your Wall Pilates practice should be too! While pre-designed routines serve as an excellent launchpad, personalizing your workouts can catapult your fitness to the next level. Here's how to make Wall Pilates truly yours.

Discover Your True North

Begin with a clarity session: What do you aim to achieve? Maybe it's better balance, core strength, or tackling specific health issues like back pain or arthritis. Once you've zoned in on your objectives, you can handpick exercises to match.

Flex Your Modification Muscles

If you've got health challenges or specific conditions, you can still do Wall Pilates—just jazz it up a bit! Got knee issues? Rethink those lunges. A certified Wall Pilates guru can help you tweak your routine so that it's both safe and effective.

Zone In: Target Training

Dreaming of a six-pack at 60 or more flexible hips? You can choose exercises that put the spotlight on your dream areas. Incorporate more plank varieties for a rock-solid core, or hip stretches for agility.

Props Aren't Just for Magicians

The wall isn't flying solo here; spice things up with some supporting acts. Resistance bands, foam rollers, and stability balls can add a new layer of intrigue and challenge.

Personalized Sample Workouts

Soothe Your Spine: Low Back Pain Routine

Exercises like Wall Planks with Leg Lifts and Wall Roll-Downs are your go-to options for relieving lower back tension and promoting spine health. Regularly performing these targeted moves can do wonders for your lower back pain while upping your flexibility game.

Steady As You Go: Balance & Stability Routine

Dive into Wall Squats and Wall Push-Ups to create a fortress of strength around your core and lower body. These aren't just exercises; they're your toolkit to prevent falls and stay agile.

Bend It Like...You! Flexibility Routine

Hips, hamstrings, and shoulders – oh my! Unleash a more flexible you with the Wall Figure Four Stretch, Wall Hamstring Stretch, and Wall Shoulder Opener. These will make you as supple as a willow in no time.

Get Your Heart Pumping: Cardiovascular Endurance

Who says cardio has to be a leap of faith? Wall-assisted variations of jumping jacks, high knees, and slow mountain climbers keep the adrenaline rush low-impact.

Flex Those Guns: Upper Body Strength Routine

Wall Push-Ups, Wall Tricep Dips, and Wall Angels are the Avengers of upper body strength. With these moves, you'll become your own superhero in no time.

Remember, there's no one-size-fits-all in Wall Pilates. By taking the reins and customizing your practice, you're not just working out; you're building a lifestyle. Always consult a Pilates professional or healthcare provider to ensure your tailored routine is both safe and kick-butt.

Chapter 7

THE EVERYDAY MAGIC OF WALL PILATES: MAKE IT A LIFESTYLE

Seamless Blending: Living the Wall Pilates Life

Look, I get it. Between errands, family, and that new Netflix series, who has the time for a full workout every day? But what if I told you Wall Pilates can blend into your life as naturally as your morning coffee? Here's how to make it happen:

Carve Out "Me Time"

First, claim your Pilates moment—set a daily alarm if you have to. Maybe it's first thing in the morning, or perhaps it's your after-dinner unwind session. Timing isn't the focus; what matters is you're making room for you.

Sneak It Into Mundane Moments

Hey, who says you can't multitask? Wall Squats while you're on a conference call? Absolutely. Wall Push-Ups while you wait for your tea to steep? Go for it! You'd be amazed at how many sneaky Pilates opportunities exist in a day.

Crank Up the Joy Factor

Turn your Wall Pilates routine into a fiesta. Get your favorite playlist going or invite a friend over for a 'Pilates and Chill' session. Maybe even throw in some Wall Plank challenges on your social media. The more fun it is, the more you'll stick with it.

Goals: Keep It Real, Keep It Rewarding

You're not training for the Pilates Olympics. Start with attainable goals—say, holding a Wall Plank for 10 seconds longer each week. Then, as you crush those goals, keep upping the ante.

Zen and the Art of Wall Pilates

Mindfulness isn't just for meditation. As you're holding that Wall Squat, tune into your body. Feel those muscles working? That's your body saying thanks. Focus on your breath, keep that spine aligned, and move with intention. You'll get a mini-mindfulness session right in the middle of your routine.

Track, Treat, Repeat

A reward system never hurt anyone, right? Keep tabs on your progress—there are even apps for that. Hit a milestone? Treat yourself! A new workout outfit or even a day off to binge-watch that Netflix series can be your reward.

Wrap Up: You Got This!

Integrating Wall Pilates into your everyday routine is way easier than you think. By setting small, doable goals, sneaking in mini-sessions, and making it all a big, joyful act, you're setting yourself up for a lifetime of better posture, stronger muscles, and a calmer mind. So, what are you waiting for? Dive into the Wall Pilates life and make it yours.

Chapter 8

Your New Beginning: Unleashing the Power of Wall Pilates

You Made It, Now Let's Celebrate You!

First off, give yourself a well-deserved pat on the back. Seriously, you've just dived deep into the wonderful world of Wall Pilates for seniors, and that's no small feat! By now, you're well-versed in the transformative perks of this practice—from boosting your strength to enhancing your balance and flexibility. And let's not forget the real MVP here: the wall, your ultimate Pilates sidekick.

Consistency is Your New Best Friend

You've probably heard it a million times, but I'll say it again: The magic happens in the everyday grind. Consistency isn't just a buzzword; it's your ticket to unlocking all the benefits Wall Pilates has to offer. Make it your daily ritual, and you'll soon see a ripple effect on your health and happiness.

Your Expanding Universe of Resources

Ready to ramp it up? The Wall Pilates cosmos is larger than you think. Whether you fancy a group vibe in a local class or want a one-on-one session with a pro, you've got options. Hey, the digital age is your playground—YouTube tutorials, specialized online courses, you name it. But remember, the green light from your healthcare provider is your golden ticket into this exciting adventure.

You're Just One Wall Away from a Healthier You

The fantastic thing about Wall Pilates is its simplicity. You don't need a fancy gym or expensive equipment. Your commitment, a sturdy wall, and a dash of enthusiasm are all you need to transform your life, one Wall Plank at a time.

A Big Thank You and a High Five!

Thank you for letting me be a part of your Wall Pilates journey. Whether you're here to build strength, improve your balance, or simply make everyday activities easier, the potential for transformation is limitless. Here's to your new, health-infused life, fueled by Wall Pilates!

Book 7

COMBINING WALL PILATES WITH OTHER FORMS OF EXERCISE

Chapter 1

The Perfect Blend—Your Introductory Guide

Hey there, and welcome to Book 7: "The Ultimate Fusion: Blending Wall Pilates with Varied Workouts." This book is your go-to manual for spicing up your Wall Pilates journey with an assortment of other fitness avenues. It's all about diversifying your workouts to unlock new levels of health and vitality. So, let's jump right in, shall we?

Power Up with Multifaceted Workouts

As we ride the wave of life, one thing is for sure—keeping a consistent exercise routine is crucial, especially in our golden years. Wall Pilates is your secret weapon for a fitter, more balanced you. But why stop there? Imagine supercharging those benefits by mixing in other workout styles! We're talking about enhanced heart health, muscle power, and limberness like never before.

The Safe Way to Mix and Match

Before you turn your exercise routine into a fitness buffet, a word of caution. Not all workout pairings are created equal, especially when we're juggling health concerns and physical limitations. But worry not, this book is your roadmap to fusion fitness that respects your unique needs, making sure you're all set for a potent yet secure exercise cocktail.

What's Cooking in the Chapters Ahead

In the chapters to follow, we'll not only delve into the science-backed benefits of combining Wall Pilates with other forms of exercise, but also arm you with safety tips tailored for seniors. Plus, I've got some killer sample workout plans to get those creative juices flowing.

So, fasten your seat belts as we venture into the exciting territory of workout alchemy!

Chapter 2

The Ultimate Yoga Fusion: Elevate Your Wall Pilates Routine

Blending Wall Pilates with Yoga isn't just an exercise upgrade; it's a lifestyle enhancement. This fusion brings together the core-centric prowess of Wall Pilates with Yoga's body-mind equilibrium. The result? A cocktail of benefits that every senior should be sipping on. So let's unpack what happens when these two powerhouse practices join forces.

Unleash the Super Benefits

- Stretch Like a Pro: Wall Pilates tunes up the suppleness in your spine, hips, and shoulders. Yoga chimes in by liberating the flexibility in literally every nook and cranny of your physique. Merged, these methods make sure you're not just aging, but "ageless-ing"!

- Stay Grounded: Talk about two-for-one: Both Wall

Pilates and Yoga are virtuosos in balance and stability. So whether you're reaching up high for that cereal box or navigating a tricky staircase, the risk of taking a spill gets knocked down a notch.

- Strength Galore: While Wall Pilates adds oomph to your core and upper body, Yoga's got your lower body all spruced up. You're not just aging stronger; you're aging smarter.

- Zen Out: Both Wall Pilates and Yoga double as stress-busting maestros, gifting you a calmer, more centered you. A daily dose of this fitness fusion can be your golden ticket to serene sunsets and unflustered mornings.

Safeguard Your Fusion Journey

Safety comes first, especially when navigating two different forms of movement. Keep these points in your pocket:

- Warm-Up Time: Kickstart your session with subtle stretches and light movements. Think of it as setting the stage for the fitness drama that's about to unfold.

- Switch 'n' Sync: Elegantly switch between Wall Pilates and Yoga postures. Dedicate a couple of minutes to one, then segue into the other. It's like dancing, but without the toe-stepping!

- Get Prop Savvy: From wall support to Yoga blocks, use props to both challenge and assist you. Props aren't cheats; they're your performance enhancers.

- Your Body, Your Rules: If something feels off, adapt. Any discomfort is your body's way of tapping out. Listen and adjust accordingly.

Sample Fusion Flows

Here are some sample routines combining Wall Pilates and Yoga:

Wall Plank Meets Downward Dog

Start with a Wall Plank, firing up your core and shoulder stability. Next, seamlessly transition into a Downward Dog. Here, you're greeting a full-body stretch while still engaging your upper body. This dynamic duo caters to muscle activation and stretchability in one go.

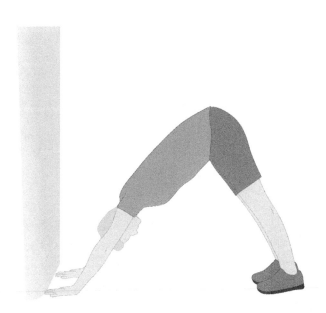

Wall Roll-Down Paired with Forward Fold

A Wall Roll-Down gives your back the pampering it needs, while a Forward Fold seals the deal with hamstring suppleness. Two different ways to achieve a comprehensive back-body stretch. Think of it as a 'hug' to your spine and hamstrings!

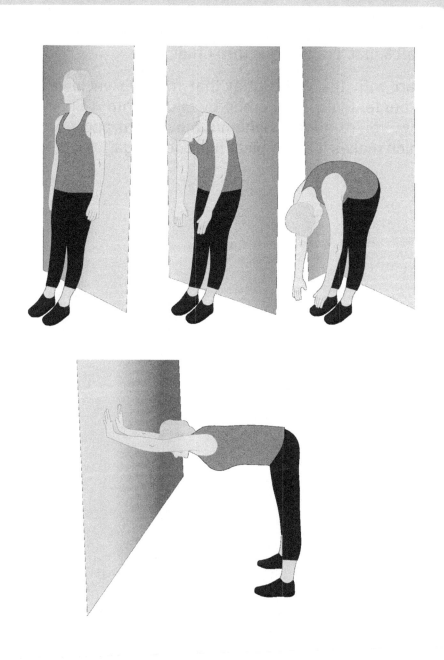

Wall Squat Transitions into Chair Pose

Start with the Wall Squat that focuses on lower-body fortitude. Make it a combo by gliding into a Chair Pose. Now, you're adding dynamic movement and arm work, which makes it a complete full-body saga.

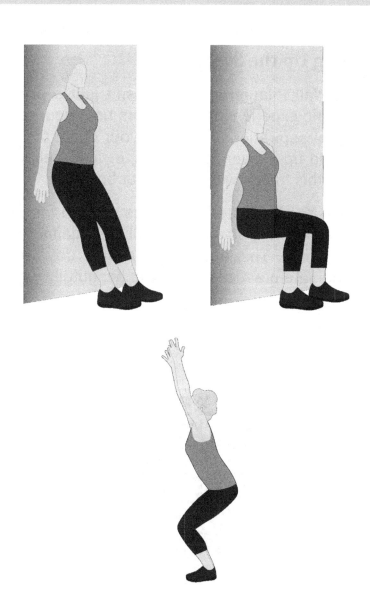

Summing Up the Symphony

Mingling Wall Pilates with Yoga isn't just a practice—it's a holistic experience that honors both your physical and mental aspirations. Whether your goals are rooted in limbering up, powering through, or just feeling more grounded, this fusion will tick all your boxes.

To explore Yoga's seated variations tailored for seniors, you might want to grab a copy of "Chair Yoga for Seniors" by Helen Stone. This book is a treasure trove of Yoga hacks and safe practices that sync beautifully with your Wall Pilates regimen.

You can get it by scanning the following QR Code:

Chapter 3

The Heart of the Matter: Wall Pilates Meets Cardio

Bored of your usual fitness routine? Blend the best of both worlds—Wall Pilates and Cardio—and you're in for a transformative health journey! The Wall Pilates focus on strength, balance, and flexibility beautifully complements the heart-pumping benefits of cardio. So let's take a look at how this dynamic duo can help you live your golden years in prime form.

The Unbeatable Benefits

• Cardio Bliss: Cardio, of course, is the go-to for pumping up your heart and lung game. But add Wall Pilates to the mix, and you're hitting a home run in all-around cardiovascular health.

• Power & Flex: With Wall Pilates in the picture, you're not just stretching—you're strengthening! The fusion offers a robust exercise regime that stretches, strengthens, and tones you up from head to toe.

• Fortify & Protect: A body tuned through Wall Pilates is better equipped to handle the rigors of cardio, reducing the risk of strain and injury. Imagine a more resilient you, ready to tackle any physical challenge!

Play It Safe and Snazzy

Embarking on this combo journey? Awesome! But let's be smart about it:

• Take Baby Steps: If you're easing back into fitness or are fresh out of a Netflix binge, let's start low-key. Begin with breezy cardio like a simple walk or a light bike ride, and escalate as you feel ready.

• Warm Up & Wind Down: No shortcut here. Both before and after your combined routine, spend time with light cardio or stretching. Think of it as the opening and closing credits for your exercise movie.

Body Talk: If your body is humming a tune of discomfort, halt and take stock. Pain isn't gain; it's a sign to step back and perhaps consult with an expert.

Sample Fusion Workouts

Wall Squats Meets Jumping Jacks

1. Start by leaning against the wall for a Wall Squat. Keep that form spot-on for 30 seconds to a minute.

2. Break free and jump into a set of Jumping Jacks, syncing your breath with each jump. Keep it going for another 30 seconds to a minute.

3. Head back to the wall for another squat.

This loop merges the toning power of squats with the calorie-burning fun of jumping jacks. You're getting a leg day and cardio blast in one go!

Wall Plank to High Knees

1. Start with your palms flat on a wall and get into a solid Wall Plank.

2. Hold the plank, then lift each knee towards your chest, as if you're running on the wall!

3. Vary the knee speed or add a resistance band for that extra spice.

This fusion works both your core stability and cardiovascular stamina, making it a sweet two-for-one deal.

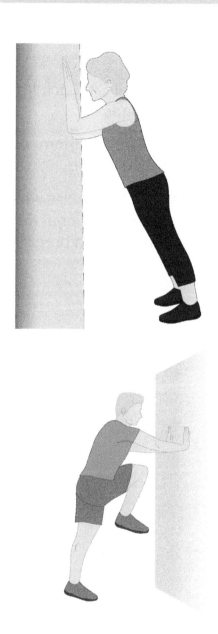

Wall Sit to Step-Ups

1. Start with your classic Wall Sit. Lock in that core and hang tight for 30-60 seconds.

2. Transition to Step-Ups. Use a platform or a sturdy box, and go for 10-15 reps on each leg.

This duo works the core and leg muscles while keeping the heart rate up. Plus, it's a great functional workout, making everyday tasks like climbing stairs a breeze.

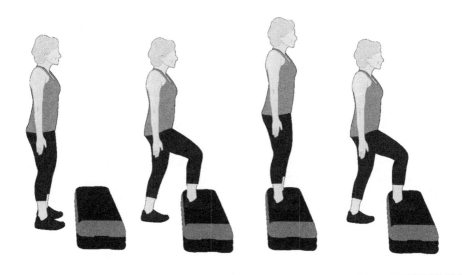

Your All-in-One Fitness Package

By fusing Wall Pilates with cardio, you're signing up for a well-rounded, versatile workout that tackles everything from your heart rate to muscle tone. It's a one-stop-shop for senior fitness that doesn't compromise on fun or functionality. However, it's always a smart idea to get a green light from your healthcare provider before hitting a new fitness milestone. So, ready to break a healthy sweat?

Chapter 4

POWER UP YOUR WALL PILATES
WITH RESISTANCE TRAINING

Ready to turbocharge your Wall Pilates game? Let's infuse some muscle-pumping resistance training into your routines! This unique combo promises to give seniors a new lease on life, from stronger bones to a well-sculpted physique. Let's jump in and see how you can make it work!

The Dynamic Duo: Wall Pilates & Resistance Training

- Stronger Bones, Happier Life: Resistance training is a secret weapon against bone density loss, a concern for many seniors. Wall Pilates brings its own set of perks, like better balance and core power.

- Flex & Stretch: Wall Pilates champions flexibility. Add resistance training to the mix, and you're talking about an entire symphony of muscle toning and stretching.

A Beginner's Guide to Mixing Wall Pilates & Resistance Training

You've got a buffet of tools like resistance bands and dumbbells to spice up your workout. Let's make sure we do it right:

Wall Squats & Dumbbell Press

1. Start in a Wall Squat pose, dumbbells in hand.

2. Power up into a standing position while pressing those dumbbells toward the ceiling.

3. Repeat for 8-10 reps.

Wall Push-Ups & Resistance Band Rows

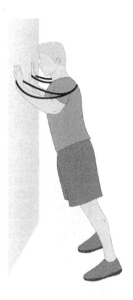

1. Set up your Wall Push-Up but add a resistance band looped around your back.

2. Push away from the wall and pull the band towards you as you go.

3. Nail this for another 8-10 reps.

Wall Roll-Down & Resistance Band Rows

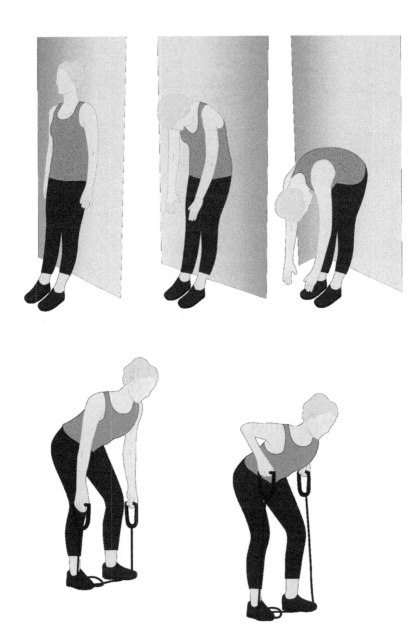

Power Up Your Wall Pilates with Resistance Training

1. Initiate a Wall Roll-Down with a resistance band gripped in your hands.

2. As you roll back up, give those resistance bands a solid row.

3. Aim for a set of 8-10 reps.

Sample Super-Routines for Seniors

Wall Squats Meet Dumbbell Press & Wall Angels

1. Get into your Wall Squat, dumbbells at the ready.

2. Press the dumbbells sky-high, then back to starting position. Go for 10 reps.

3. With arms out and parallel to the ground, perform Wall Angels for another 10 reps.

Perform 3 complete sets.

The key? Choose the right dumbbell weight for you and find that sweet spot distance from the wall.

Wall Push-Ups & Resistance Band Rows + Wall Roll-Downs

1. Set up your Wall Push-Up but add a resistance band looped around your back.

2. Perform a Wall Push-Up while engaging with the band, aiming for 8-10 reps.

3. Shift to Wall Roll-Down, pulling off rows with the band as you rise. Repeat for another 8-10 reps.

These routines blend upper body sculpting with Wall Pilates' core stability, making them perfect for a holistic workout.

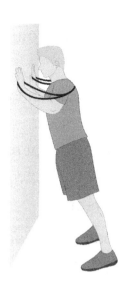

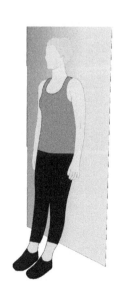  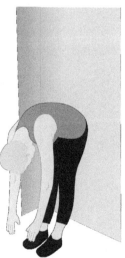

Wall Planks with Tricep Extensions + Wall Squats with Bicep Curls

1. Get into Wall Plank mode, holding a resistance band in your hands.

2. Engage your core and hold that straight line.

3. Squat down, pulling off a bicep curl as you go, and then rise back up for 8-10 reps.

These sets are for those who want a bolder workout, focusing on arm and shoulder strength while still working on core and balance.

The Full-Circle Fitness Experience

So there you have it—a Wall Pilates and resistance training mash-up that offers the best of both worlds. It's like having your cake and eating it too, except here, you're actually burning calories and building muscle. As always, give your healthcare provider a shout before diving into a new routine, just to get that medical thumbs-up. Ready to elevate your fitness? Let's crush it!

Chapter 5

HARMONIZE YOUR BODY AND MIND WITH WALL PILATES AND TAI CHI

Ready to supercharge your wellness journey? Let's talk about how Wall Pilates and Tai Chi can be your twin saviors, like a fitness version of yin and yang. One brings you robust strength and flexibility, the other soothes your mind and soul. When we combine them, the synergy is transformative. Let's explore how!

The Yin and Yang of Wall Pilates and Tai Chi

Tai Chi is often called "meditation in motion," and it's the perfect complement to Wall Pilates. Together, they create a holistic wellness package that includes:

- Rock-Solid Balance: Both Wall Pilates and Tai Chi are MVPs when it comes to balance. Fuse them together, and you've got an ultimate defense against trips and falls.

- Flex Those Muscles: Both methods emphasize slow, intentional movements that are like a balm for your flexibility and range of motion. You'll be reaching for the top shelf in no time!

- Peace of Mind: Tai Chi melts stress while Wall Pilates helps you find your center. Together, they're a mental health powerhouse. Say goodbye to restless nights!

Wall Pilates + Tai Chi = Your New Routine

Let's get you started with some fun and safe routines. Remember, it's a marathon, not a sprint, so pace yourself!

- Warm-up: Kickstart your session with Wall Pilates essentials like Wall Angels and Wall Roll-Downs. Think of it as the appetizer before the main course.

- Tai Chi Essentials: Step into basic Tai Chi moves like the Tai Chi stance or Tai Chi Walk. You'll be focusing on breathing and posture, laying a strong foundation for what's to come.

- The Fusion: Start incorporating Wall Pilates moves into your Tai Chi flow. Imagine doing Wall Squats with Arm Extensions while holding a Tai Chi stance. It's like adding a shot of espresso to your latte!

Sample Combo Routines for Maximum Bliss

Tai Chi Stance Meets Wall Squats

1. Stand facing the wall, hands at shoulder height, feet shoulder-width apart.

2. Shift one foot back and rotate it slightly outward.

3. Squat down, balancing your weight between both feet.

4. Rise slowly and repeat.

Feel your leg muscles engage while your mind remains focused. It's all about equilibrium!

Wall Planks Jive with Tai Chi Walk

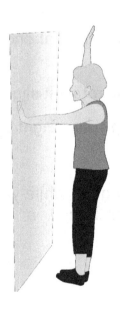

1. Start in a Wall Plank position, keeping your core tight.

2. Lift one hand toward the ceiling.

3. Return to the Wall Plank position and repeat on the other side.

Your core and shoulders will thank you, and you'll feel as graceful as a Tai Chi master!

Wall Sit Finds Zen with Tai Chi Arm Raises

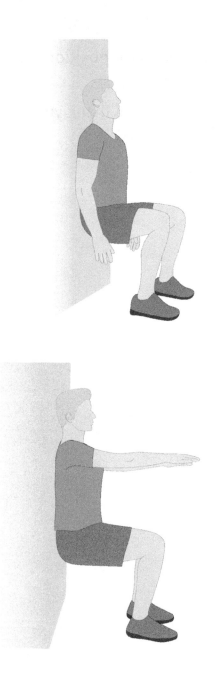

Harmonize Your Body and Mind with Wall Pilates and Tai Chi

1. Slide down into a Wall Sit, knees bent at 90 degrees.

2. Extend your arms out with palms facing down.

3. Slowly raise your arms to shoulder height, then bring them back down.

You're not just toning your legs and arms; you're practicing mindful movement.

Final Thoughts: Your Road to Holistic Wellness

Marrying Wall Pilates with Tai Chi is like putting two superheroes in the same room: You're bound to get something extraordinary. Your balance, flexibility, and mental well-being will all experience a fantastic boost. But remember, whether you're a fitness rookie or an experienced athlete, always consult your healthcare provider before trying out new routines. Get ready to embark on a transformative journey of harmonious living!

Chapter 6

Unlock Your Full Potential with Wall Pilates and Stretching

Hey there, fitness enthusiasts! Let's dive into a chapter that promises to loosen up those tight muscles and joints we often collect over the years. Think of Wall Pilates and stretching as a dynamic duo—your body's very own Batman and Robin. By bringing them together, you can target just about any muscle group and do wonders for your flexibility and range of motion.

The Golden Benefits: Wall Pilates + Stretching

Melding Wall Pilates with stretching and mobility work can supercharge your wellness journey. Here's what you get:

- Unleash Flexibility: We're talking limber muscles and easy movement. Say hello to touching your toes again!

- Motion is the Potion: Boost that range of motion to keep you agile, enhancing your quality of life and even making those household chores a breeze.

- Bye-Bye, Stiffness: No more waking up feeling like the Tin Man from "The Wizard of Oz." This combo will leave your muscles relaxed and ready for action.

- Stand Tall: Ever catch yourself slumping? These routines can seriously uplift your posture, reducing the risk of falls and enhancing your silhouette.

How to Blend Wall Pilates and Stretching Like a Pro

Okay, you're sold on the why, but what about the how? Let's ensure you're stretching with smarts and style:

- Warm It Up: A few rounds of Wall Roll-Downs and Wall Angels will get your muscles eager for action.

- Wall Support: Leverage the wall to deepen your stretches. It's like having a personal assistant who's always there for you!

- Mindful Movements: Make each move a meditation. Breathe deeply and give each stretch the time it deserves.

- Body Talk: Listen to what your muscles and joints are saying. Pain means it's time to pause.

Sample Fusion Routines: Stretching Meets Wall Pilates

Wall Squats Meet Hip Openers

1. Stand against the wall, hands and feet shoulder-width apart.

2. Slide down into a squat.

3. Stand back up and lift your right knee towards your chest.

4. Open that knee sideways, like you're a dog at a fire hydrant.

5. Bring it back, set it down, and switch legs.

Feel that? Your hips are saying thank you!

Wall Angels Pair with Shoulder Stretches

1. Stand against the wall, arms at your sides.

2. Raise your arms to form a 'W' against the wall.

3. Glide your arms up the wall, palms forward, then back down.

4. Interlace your fingers behind you.

5. Gently lift your arms for a delicious chest and shoulder stretch.

It's like giving your upper body a mini-vacation!

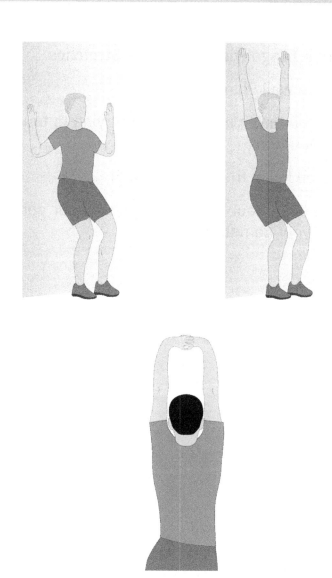

Wall Planks Tango with Hamstring Stretches

1. Assume a Wall Plank.

2. Extend your arms and lift one leg trying to touch your heel to your rear.

3. Hold, then lower the leg and switch.

This move does double duty: It torches your core while pampering your hamstrings.

Wrapping It Up: Your Guide to Better Living

Combining Wall Pilates with stretching and mobility work is like adding a turbo booster to your fitness rocket ship. You're set for an exhilarating ride toward better health, lower injury risk, and an amazing quality of life. But remember, before you set sail on any new fitness adventure, it's always good to get a nod from your healthcare provider. Happy stretching!

Chapter 7

Your Personal Blueprint for Fitness Success

Welcome back, fitness aficionados! Ready to up the ante? Let's craft your perfect Wall Pilates routine that seamlessly blends with other fabulous exercises you love. It's all about building an exercise regimen that feels like it's tailor-made for you—because it is!

Shape Your Mission

Think of your fitness journey as an epic saga. What's your endgame? Is it flexing stronger muscles, nailing that dancer-like flexibility, or becoming so balanced you could give a tightrope walker a run for their money? Having razor-sharp goals helps you reverse-engineer your exercise plan for undeniable success.

Know Thyself: Take a Fitness Selfie

Time for some real talk. How fit are you—right here, right now? A truthful assessment helps lay the groundwork. You'll zero in on the ideal blend of exercises, and figure out how to dial the intensity up or down. This is your reality check; think of it as your fitness "before" pic.

The Perfect Mix: Wall Pilates Plus What?

With your goals and current fitness level in your back pocket, let's curate that ideal exercise playlist. Want more balance? Spice up Wall Pilates with a side of Tai Chi or some balancing yoga poses. Craving strength? Consider adding in resistance training or even some cardio blasts. Your menu, your choice!

The Nitty-Gritty: How Often and How Long?

Just like you wouldn't binge-watch an entire TV series in one night (or would you?), it's key to set a sustainable frequency and duration for your workouts. Are we talking short daily sessions or longer, less frequent bursts? The trick is to make it challenging enough to see progress but sustainable enough that you won't hit the burnout.

The Progress Diaries: Celebrate Your Wins!

You wouldn't embark on a cross-country road trip without a GPS, right? Keep tabs on your journey by jotting down your workouts and noting your small victories along the way. Whether it's shaving seconds off your Wall Plank time or mastering a complex Tai Chi sequence, these wins become the breadcrumbs on your trail to success. It's your motivation jet fuel!

Final Thoughts: Your Blueprint, Your Rules

Crafting a tailor-made exercise plan isn't just a roadmap to your fitness goals; it's your personal blueprint for a healthier, more vibrant you. As your own architect, you have the freedom to tweak, adjust, and redefine your plan as you see fit. Because at the end of the day, you're not just building a workout routine; you're constructing a lifestyle.

And remember, if you're making a significant change to your routine or have any health concerns, always run it by your healthcare provider. With their thumbs-up, you're good to go—straight towards your healthiest self!

Here are some sample exercise plans for different ability levels:

Beginner plan

- 10 minutes of Wall Pilates exercises (such as Wall Roll-Downs and Wall Angels)

- 10 minutes of low-impact cardiovascular exercise (such as walking or stationary cycling)

- 5 minutes of stretching and mobility exercises (such as Wall Squats with Hip Openers and Wall Angels with Shoulder Stretches)

- Frequency: 3-4 times per week

Intermediate plan

- 20 minutes of Wall Pilates exercises (such as Wall Squats with Dumbbell Press and Wall Planks with

Resistance Band Tricep Extensions)

- 20 minutes of moderate-intensity cardiovascular exercise (such as swimming or brisk walking)
- Stretching and mobility drills for 10 minutes, such as wall planks with hamstring stretches and wall angels with shoulder stretches
- Frequency: 4-5 times per week

Advanced plan

- 30 minutes of Wall Pilates exercises (such as Wall Squats with Resistance Band Bicep Curls and Wall Planks with Tai Chi Walk)
- 30 minutes of high-intensity cardiovascular exercise (such as running or cycling)
- 15 minutes of stretching and mobility exercises (such as Wall Squats with Hip Openers and Wall Planks with Hamstring Stretches)
- Frequency: 5-6 times per week

Absolutely, you've hit the nail on the head! Your health and safety should always be priority numero uno. Before diving into your newly minted, super-personalized workout plan, get that all-important green light from your healthcare provider. They can offer invaluable insights tailored to your medical history and current condition.

As you go along, always remember to keep the conversation with your body open. Experiencing some discomfort or, heaven forbid, pain? Take that as a sign to pause, recalibrate, or perhaps consult with a fitness or medical expert for tweaks to your regimen.

Here's the bottom line: A personalized exercise cocktail that marries Wall Pilates with other enriching activities offers you a golden ticket to a vibrant, dynamic life in your golden years. It's not just about adding years to your life, but life to your years!

So gear up, listen to your body, and forge ahead toward an active, balanced, and joyful life. With a well-rounded and customized plan, you're not just surviving; you're thriving, my friend!

Chapter 8

YOUR QUESTIONS ANSWERED

When it comes to blending Wall Pilates with other workout styles, let's just say seniors have the ultimate fitness smorgasbord right at their fingertips! But like any all-you-can-eat buffet, you've got questions about what to put on your plate. Here, we'll spill the tea on your most burning questions to set you up for ultimate workout success.

Q: Is it cool to mix Wall Pilates with other workouts?

A: Absolutely, yes! You're more than safe mixing up Wall Pilates with other exercise modalities, as long as you keep a few key points in mind. Dial-in on your form, kick things off gently, and ramp up gradually as you grow stronger. Oh, and don't forget—your healthcare provider should be in the loop before you embark on any new fitness journey.

Q: Can I mesh Wall Pilates with high-octane stuff like running or jumping?

A: You bet! If you're into the adrenaline-pumping, heart-thumping stuff, you can absolutely combine it with the more Zen vibes of Wall Pilates. Just remember to start easy, and as your stamina builds, feel free to crank up the intensity. A pro tip? Invest in some good kicks and consider softer surfaces to treat your joints like the VIPs they are.

Q: How many Wall Pilates sessions should I sneak into my week?

A: It's your call! The "magic number" varies depending on your goals and where you're starting from, fitness-wise. However, a solid rule of thumb is to aim for at least 30 minutes of some kind of exercise most days. You can infuse Wall Pilates into this framework as much as you like, just remember: everyone—including you—needs a little R&R between workouts.

Q: How can I tell if I'm going too hard?

A: Listen to your body's SOS. If you're pushing too hard, you might feel chest pain, find it tough to catch your breath, get dizzy, or even feel like you're running on empty. Any of these are your body's way of saying, "Hey, slow down there, champ!" Take it seriously and seek medical advice ASAP.

Q: What if I've got some pre-existing health drama?

A: Get an all-clear. If you've got an ongoing medical condition, having a chat with your healthcare provider is a non-negotiable first step. They can steer you towards what's safe and perhaps offer exercise hacks customized just for you.

Q: How do I make sure my workout has all the bells and whistles?

A: Go for the trifecta. A rockstar workout hits all your major muscle groups, revs up your heart rate, and throws in some stretches and balance work for good measure. If you're feeling a little lost in the fitness sauce, don't hesitate to consult with a certified fitness expert or rely on vetted exercise programs to craft a well-rounded routine.

By tackling these FAQs head-on, you're well on your way to creating a foolproof, super-charged fitness regimen that beautifully melds Wall Pilates with other forms of exercise. Your golden years are about to get a whole lot more golden!

Chapter 9

Your Roadmap to Lifelong Wellness

High-fives all around—you've just powered through the ins and outs of crafting your own Wall Pilates-infused workout routine! It's like having a spice rack of wellness options tailored just for you. Whether your jam is flexibility, balance, or all-around fitness, you've got the tools to take your health game to the next level.

Keep it Real and Keep Listening

As you lace up those sneakers and embark on your personal fitness quest, always remember: your body's feedback is the ultimate compass. Tune into its signals and tweak your routine accordingly. If you've got questions or bump into any roadblocks, don't hesitate to bring in the pros—like your healthcare provider—for some expert advice.

Your Fitness Toolbox

To keep your wellness journey fresh and fun, consider

adding these resources to your arsenal:

Local Hotspots

Check out local gyms or community centers, many of which offer eclectic exercise classes that throw Wall Pilates into the mix. It's not just about the workout—it's a cool way to connect with like-minded folks in your community.

Digital Fitness Buffet

Cyberspace is chock-full of workout inspo. Whether you're a YouTube fitness guru follower or swear by subscription services like Pilates Anytime or Daily Burn, there's something for everyone. Plus, it's a great way to keep your routine spicy from the comfort of your home.

Your Personal Fitness Sidekick

If you're in the mood for some VIP treatment, consider hiring a personal trainer or a fitness coach. They can offer one-on-one advice, motivation, and even tailor exercises to fit your individual needs.

Stay Committed and Keep Rockin' It

At the end of the day, your wellness journey is a marathon, not a sprint. Consistency is your bestie here. Make fitness a non-negotiable in your calendar, and before you know it, you'll not only hit those goals but probably set some new ones that you hadn't even imagined.

Best of luck, and here's to the exciting fitness adventures that await you!

The Ultimate Bundle Wrap-Up

Hey there, Wellness Warrior,

Wow, you did it! You've just wrapped up an entire bundle of seven enriching books on Wall Pilates for seniors, and that's no small feat. Your pursuit of this knowledge speaks volumes about your commitment to living your best, healthiest life—and let me tell you, that's something to be proud of.

Your Wellness Journey, Unpacked

This series wasn't just a collection of tips and exercises—it was your blueprint to unlock a new level of wellness. It's like having a toolbox where each book is a new tool to amplify your health.

- Book 1: Laid down the ABCs of Pilates, unraveling its fascinating history and foundational principles. You learned why Pilates is a game-changer for seniors.

- Books 2 & 3: Took you on a tour of standing and seated Wall Pilates exercises, shaping the way you think about stability, posture, and balance. You even had some fun with warm-ups and cool-downs.

- Book 4: Turned up the heat with props like balls and bands, taking your flexibility and strength to new heights.

- Book 5: Unleashed more advanced exercises to level up your balance, coordination, and overall mojo, complete with cool-down routines for that post-workout glow.

- Book 6: Offered curated Wall Pilates routines for various fitness levels and showed you how to tweak them to suit your unique needs.

- Book 7: The grand finale! Merged Wall Pilates with a kaleidoscope of other activities, from yoga and cardio to resistance training, Tai Chi, and stretching. Plus, you walked away with the know-how to craft your personalized workout agenda.

Your Road Ahead

As you've seen, Wall Pilates is like the Swiss army knife of wellness for seniors. It bolsters everything from your posture to your mental well-being and even helps you sidestep those pesky injuries. The wall isn't just a wall; it's your new best gym buddy!

The journey isn't over; it's only just begun. Consistency is your ticket to an active and invigorating life. Be bold, try new routines, and don't hesitate to blend Wall Pilates with other forms of exercise you enjoy.

To Infinity and Beyond

Thanks for entrusting your wellness journey to this series. The investment you've made in your health will pay off in spades, not just in years added to your life, but in life added to your years.

Cheers to your next chapter in health and happiness!

Stay fabulous,

Clara Hanson